D0106337

THE TRAIL H

THE
TRAIL
HOME

Nature, Imagination,
and the American West

John Daniel

PANTHEON BOOKS
New York and San Francisco

Originally published in hardcover, in slightly different form, by Pantheon Books, a division of Random House, Inc., in 1992.

Some essays in this work were originally published as follows: "The Garden and the Field": *North American Review,* Fall 1989 · "The Impoverishment of Sightseeing": *Wilderness* Magazine, Fall 1990 · "On the Power of Wild Water" originally published in different form as "Water Power": *Wilderness* Magazine, Winter 1986 · "The Long Dance of the Trees" originally published in different form: *Wilderness* Magazine, Spring 1988 · "Desert Walking": *Southwest Review,* Spring 1992 · "Remembering the Sacred Family" originally published in different form: *Orion,* Summer 1990 · "The Poem of Being": *Epoch,* 141:2 Spring 1992 · "Some Mortal Speculations": *Wilderness* Magazine, Summer 1989 · "The Trail Home": *North American Review,* Summer 1991 · "Among Animals": excerpted originally in *Left Bank,* Spring 1992. · "Wallace Stegner" originally published in different form: *Bloomsbury Review,* July/August 1993 · "The Limits of Paradise" originally published in different form: *Sierra* Magazine, March/April 1994.

Acknowledgments to reprint previously published material may be found on page 265.

Library of Congress Cataloging-in-Publication Data
Daniel, John, 1948–
    The trail home: nature, imagination, and the American West/John Daniel.
        p.   cm.
    ISBN 0-679-75438-5
    1. Nature.   2. Natural history.   3. Man—Influence on nature.   I. Title.
QH81.D19   1992
508—dc20   91–50752

DESIGN BY LAURA HOUGH
Manufactured in the United States of America
First Revised Edition
9   8   7   6   5   4   3   2   1

For Wallace Stegner,
with thanks for his example
as writer, conservationist,
and human being

Contents

Contents

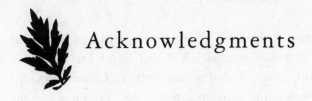

Acknowledgments

I'VE HAD PLENTY of helpful company in the making of this book. My desert rambles with Bruce Bowerman, a scientist who reads poetry, have nourished several of the essays. Roger Smith enlightened me on points of both language and science, and bolstered my spirits with afternoons of beer and good talk. Scott Slovic has been an energetic advocate of my work and of nature writing itself. I've valued the friendly interest of David Brower and my membership in his extended family. Jeffrey Harrison, Ehud Havazelet, Kenneth Margolis, and Aina Niemela have all given sound advice on one or more of the essays.

From the beginning, the criticism of W. S. Di Piero has been as good as his cooking, and as encouraging. Kenneth Fields introduced me to Native American literatures and to a new standard of brilliance in teaching. T. H. Watkins, editor of *Wilderness,* has been generous with space for my work, and writes some of the liveliest letters in my mail. Jim Hepworth included me early on in his field of enthusiasm, helped me believe I was writing a book, and guided it toward publication. North Point Press provided one grant-in-aid, and Roy and Rebecca Conant provided another—a job in their good book store. I did much of the later work while writer-in-residence at Austin Peay State University, in Clarksville, Tennessee, where David Till, Malcolm Glass, and many others, faculty and students, made me feel at home.

My editors, Jack Shoemaker and Dominique Gioia, have rewarded my faith at every turn. I hope I can reward theirs as amply.

Wallace and Mary Stegner shared not only their counsel, encouragement, and good company, but also the landscape where the trail of this book began.

From Wendell Berry I learn continually the meanings of work, responsibility, and hope. Some of the defects of these essays can be traced to the fact that I haven't listened to him well enough.

My mother, Zilla Hawes Daniel, opened my awareness to nature when I was a boy, and read the proofs of this book with her usual care and thoughtfulness.

Marilyn, my wife, gave the steadiest and most generous help of all. I might have been able to do it without her, but it's hard to imagine how. Through her love, forbearance, and support, she has made the writing of this book one of the pleasurable possibilities of our marriage.

THE TRAIL HOME

The Garden and the Field

APRIL EIGHTEENTH

I am staring at clods. Seventy square feet of hard-baked, indestructible dobe clods. Pound two of them together and a little dust drifts off. Isn't the way of things *away* from rocks, toward pebbles and grains of sand, toward good loose *dirt?* Why does dirt solidify to cloddy stones in my back yard? Probably I should empty the redwood frame of this alleged soil and fill it with topsoil and bark litter, plastic-bagged at Payless. But the hackles of self-sufficiency rise. A few phrases rattle in my mind, practically my entire supply of gardening knowledge: *Work the ground to a depth of two feet. Plant one inch deep in good loose soil. . . .* I will work the ground. I will split these stones so that seeds may nestle in a cushy bed and send their little feeders easily down and raise the seedling, shouldering its way and shedding the earth crumbs. So that Robert Frost may have written the truth. So that something will *grow,* damn it.

An hour later, the day is hotter and I am on closer terms with my local ground. I am grating clods across a heavy wire screen laid over the wheelbarrow, milling them into dry dirt. They don't mill easily. It takes all my strength focused down to the heels of both hands, a clod in each hand, four or five grates across the screen—raising an awful racket on a perfectly peaceful Sunday afternoon—and even with all of that, some of them won't crumble completely. An irreducible nucleus remains, vibrating my leather-gloved palms. They could tip drill bits with the stuff. I toss these atoms into the field and scoop up more clods.

The field is a useful place to live next to. I throw lots of things there: sticks I manage to see before mowing over them, rotten lemons off the tree, brush and pruned limbs, organic garbage from the cottage. The field absorbs it all. In late October, after the rains have begun, it greens up with its regular crop of wild oats and mustard. No one plows it, no one works the ground, it just happens. By March the mustard is four feet tall and opening into yellow bloom, rank and brilliant in the sun, at dusk an entire hillside of gently radiant light. Deer browse through, the resident red-shouldered hawk flaps over with its yelping cries, once in a while a scruffy coyote lopes along the firebreak. The field continues, with me or without me. The field has always been my idea of a garden—a place that takes care of itself, where what rises is good, and goes on.

But the field doesn't raise tomatoes, which is why I am grating clods into dust and clearing my sinuses with sneezes. It doesn't raise beans and carrots and cucumbers and lettuce. Those words must be placed in the mouth of the earth. And the earth must be cultivated, like anyone who would speak well, if it is to utter the sweet language of summer produce. I am sick of the banalities spoken in supermarkets. I write poems and I want poems to eat, rich red suns of August. The narrow redwood frame is already in place, the sun exposure is good, the time of year is right, I am filled with ambition and seed-packet wisdom—but I wasn't counting on clods.

Suddenly, as my sweat falls on the screen, I am inspired. I drop my burden and go for the hose. If you can't grate the damn things, melt them. The dry clay turns rich brown under the spray, looks better already. My wife comes up from the cottage to help, amused by my noise and commotion. Things are definitely improving. Marilyn keeps the spray going while I put a few wet clods to the screen—immediately the mesh is clogged with mud, as if I were grating soft cheese. A smear of sticky ooze, stones of still-dry clay. Evening, the first day. And not much good.

APRIL TWENTY-SECOND

We rent our cottage from Wally and Mary, who settled on this hill forty years ago. I don't know when they started the compost pile, but it must have been long ago. It's a haystack heap, spilling over the buckling wire fence that tries to hold it in. Spading aside the upper layers

3

of leaf debris and flattened sheaves of grass, I dig down through cross-hatchings of sticks, resistant orange and grapefruit peels, deposits of crunched eggshells, the various elements growing less distinct as I descend. Here, the local and the exotic melt together: native blue oak leaves commingle with Salvadoran banana peels, petals of California poppy with tea leaves from Ceylon, eucalyptus and Japanese maple with Colombian coffee grounds and bread crusts that were once Kansas wheat, all of it going over to the dark matrix, the nation of decay.

Four feet down I come to the real stuff, the crumbling black lode spotted with films of mold. It exhales a cool dank breath in my face. Worms wave their heads, or tails, in the startling light—semaphores, the news from four feet under. Here is pure potential, the unconscious of the earth, the formless stuff that all forms rise from. Maybe stirring this will stir my own imagination, dull and fruitless these days. I dredge the compost across the screen, humming happily, filling fat wheelbarrow loads of the rich concoction of death.

Worked into my grated dobe and spread across the framed plot, its charcoal black softened to chocolate brown in the glare of sun, the compost moves. It shifts and wiggles, it squirms. Sow bugs, centipedes, earwigs, spiders, more creatures than I'll ever have names for, crawl among one another, all over the soil, a shifting weave of motion that makes me blink my eyes and squint. I never saw them as I dug the stuff from the pit. A good sign, I guess. Fertile ground. But not exactly the forms I had in mind. Aren't these critters here to *eat?* And I'm entrusting my seeds to them? My tomato plants? My red suns of August?

APRIL TWENTY-SIXTH

Drop in the seed, cover it, pat the warm earth down. Water it black. What else? Roethke heard the sucking and sobbing of cuttings putting down roots, resurrecting themselves. I hear nothing from these seeds and spindly tomato plants. But I do like sitting here in the evening air, watching the wet soil, knowing it's primed with hours of my work and its own latent power. Drop in the seed and the dirt takes over, the moist warmth, the dark. It's mystery now, out of my hands. But I want to follow. I want to understand what begins to wake the seeds. I want to hear that inaudible moan or hum, that chant of all the lives and parts of lives the dirt composes—I hear it after all, in my mind—that steady call, alive down there, that cannot rise without the seeds, that even now enfolds them with its infinitesimal vibration, urging them *remember now, remember now, it is time to remember yourself* . . .

MAY TENTH

The second wilting-hot day in a row, and all along the length of the frame the beans are popping up. They rise, hunched over, the cotyledon lifting itself so fast you can almost see it happen, splitting open to issue the first pair of heart-shaped leaves. The sprouts shrug off the weight of whatever clods or sticks overlie them, they straighten themselves and say Beans! to the sun. Yesterday they were only suspicious upwellings of soil. Today the tallest are two inches high, the cotyledon split wide like two mittened hands, the bumpy twin leaves fully unfurled and already drilled here and there with insect holes.

The lemon cucumbers sprout with less exuberance, each with a pair of stout round leaves like football shoulder pads. One morning they appear, then for days they seem to wait, one inch tall. Startled by the light? Gathering strength for the charge into vinehood? Whatever they're doing, there's something proper about their appearance. The two-leafed tops have a capable air, seeming poised to push on, yet respectful of the new world they find themselves in. They make neither a grand entrance nor a meek one. They rise appropriately.

MAY TWELFTH

The poet wrote, "Before I built a wall I'd ask to know / What I was walling in or walling out." Me, I don't have to ask. Except for Wally and Mary, whose house is just uphill from ours, our closest neighbors are the deer. They bed and browse in the field, and as we walk the trail between our cottage and our cars we see them through the oaks walking their parallel trail, just down the slope. We see them, though of course they've seen us first. Deer and humans stop to stare at each other, then pass on. It's a good relationship: we enjoy their company, and they at least tolerate ours.

But as spring turns to summer and summer settles in to its hot blue eternity, the green field goes bleached gold, all brittle stems and husks, and the deer want to be closer friends. We wake to find them tearing grass between the cottage and the house, or nibbling impatiens by our front door. They are not shy guests. If the flowers were inside and the door open, we would find them in the living room. They regard us with mild interest, ears erect, ink-smudge noses poised our way a moment before they turn to browse again. If we move too suddenly, they tense—forelegs spread stiffly—and bound off down the hill in elegant mincing hops.

Flowers are small-time, a frill. Though Marilyn is less generous, perhaps because she planted them, I am glad for the deer to have their share. They are lifelong residents here, after all, while we are only visitors. But now that I am spending the sweat of my own brow to till the earth, now that the lines of little green shoots and pert tomato plants are fairly leaping—much to my astonishment—under my loving hand, now it is time to make good neighbors of the deer. Attentive listeners that they are, they must be made to understand that the beans are shouting for me, not for them. If they do not recognize the difference between garden and field, I am here to instruct them with a six-foot sheepwire fence.

MAY TWENTY-THIRD

For several days a gopher has been burrowing around inside the fence and just outside the garden frame, a foot away from my lacy carrots and tender, starting-to-sprawl cucumber vines. He doesn't know how close he is to bonanza, but I do. I've been poking a hose into the loose earth he mounds up, feeling for the hard-to-find hole in order to flood his chambers. Each morning I find fresh mounds of fine granular dobe.

This morning I stick the hose in a crack at the base of the frame and instantly he appears, sprung full-blown from the earth, his gray-brown coat slightly lighter than the color of the ground. We are both too startled to move. He seems almost not to have eyes, they are so low on his face and so down-gazing. But more than I want to stare at him, I want this chewing machine away from my garden. I prod with a stick and he scuttles along the redwood, not fast, but steady. Everything he comes to he tries to go *under*—wisps of dead grass, a piece of board, various clods and stones. There is nothing cool and massy he can get his snout and shoulders beneath; he is drowning in openness. I herd him along, under the deer fence and out into the field. In the firebreak he rustles around beneath a thatch of golden grass. Relentless scourge, I prod him deeper into the field. Not much green to eat out here, but he'll have to make do.

In a niche among the black rocky clods he starts his digging. He snouts down and loosens dirt with his long, powerful forepaws; then, instead of flicking it backwards out of the hole in the style of dogs, he turns himself around and pushes the dirt out ahead of him with a rapid shuffling of paws. He shuffles so fast and hard his whole body seems to vibrate, then after two or three shuffles he faces into his hole again. Quickly and steadily he works, facing down, facing up, raising a mound of pulverized clay as he digs deeper.

Though I know he'll be back to my garden tomorrow, I feel a great refreshment in watching him. It's the pleasure of witnessing work well-performed, a creature doing what it is well-suited to do. This gopher sinks himself into ground as ably, as gracefully, as a wren constructs its nest, as a salmon fans silt from her spawning gravel, as a carpenter hammers home his nails. I would like to express myself as naturally and utterly as the gopher digs his way home. I would like to throw myself so industriously to my work. Gophers dig. Writers write, or should.

Within a couple of minutes I can see no part of him, only a recurrent spume of earth. And then the hole itself disappears: there is only the mound, trembling slightly now and then with an energy from below. My gopher has escaped the seared field to the coolness of clay. The light no longer stings his eyes. The proper aura of earthsmell has returned around him, the mild pressure on hide and whiskers. He has returned to the solid sea where he swims and swims, and every direction he swims is right.

JUNE EIGHTH

This evening I walk right under one of the two young great horned owls. He is in the big white oak near the center of the field. Streaked white and tawny, fat with juvenile feathers, his two emerging devil's horns barely visible, he gazes placidly with half-open eyes. There is no fear in him, nor is he interested in me. He is as plump and calm as Buddha.

Now another owl, an adult I hadn't seen, swoops out of the oak, dips low across the field of sere oats, and rises into a tall eucalyptus. The fledgling pushes from the limb and flaps and glides across the field to his mother.

Since I first noticed them several weeks ago, drawn by their insistent raspy whistles, I haven't seen either of the young ones flying from tree to tree, only hopping and fluttering from limb to limb of this spacious oak, testing their wings. Now and then I saw one or the other try to light on too flimsy a perch—the twig would arc precariously, the little owl flapping strenuously to stay upright, then finding surer footing closer in to the trunk or dropping to a lower limb. They are born with a genius, but like any genius it needs practice. The oak is their jungle gym. Now one of them, at least, has launched from his learning tree into the gulf of evening air. Having watched him these weeks, I am exhilarated. And the owl? To him, perhaps it is nothing so remarkable. The rush of air, the glide on outstretched wings, the field passing beneath him—it is merely the next thing he does. He was born to fly, and now he flies.

JUNE TWENTY-EIGHTH

It is clear that the cucumbers own the garden. The frilly carrots are no competition: neat in their rows, they want only to wave their ostrich plumes. They know their place, as do the beans, which cling to the fence. The tomatoes, braced and channeled up by the lath frame I build as they grow, flourish higher than the cucumbers, and showier too, with their fruit now starting to flush orange and pink. They seem to dominate the little oblong plot. But the lemon cucumbers, sprawling along the ground, unframed and uncontained, are more serious, more lushly aggressive. Fuzzy five-pointed leaves are uncrinkling every day, flopping open in frank sensual abandon. Brash with sun the curly vines extend themselves, circling so thickly among one another that the six plants make one—one leafy tangle thickening out of the ground, harboring yellow blossoms and button-yellow fruit in the cool of its shade. Near the base of each fattening vinestalk, unnotable and practically unnoticeable, those two initial shoulder-pad leaves remain, yellowed and partly eaten, about to slough off—

the first line of the first draft, the leaves that led this extravagance to light. And all along the vines, thin pale tendrils
are reaching and reaching, curling and coiling around what
is there—fencewire, tops of the carrots, sticks and clods—
whatever purchase they can find, on thing or empty air, to
help them haul from the seed's split throat the entire
shouted cucumber song of their growing.

JULY SEVENTEENTH

Like the owls, only not so alert, I wake up in
the evening. I see best then, in my way of seeing. At
sundown, as the day's light cools and swallows begin to fly
in the field, my awareness sharpens. A breeze shimmers the
dry wild oats. Two scrub jays, raucous all day with their
harsh cries, sit quietly on the phone wire, soft blue in the
slant sunlight. A mourning dove calls. Each sound, each
thing, seems now imbued with significance more than its
own—or entirely its own, as if each now achieves its complete being, no longer bleached in the day's glaring light
and drowned in its noisiness. Done with mowing, done
with weeding the garden, done with writing that isn't
going well, in this moment I want only to let my consciousness roam freely in the field, enveloping the oaks, sifting
through grasses like the soft wind, of its own accord, no
more mine than the wind is mine. What I call mine, what
I call mind, is a light I borrow from the light of sky. And
as the change comes to sky and field, the last shadows

blending into dusk, the clarity of things dissolving, darkness composing itself, the only light left is that glowing within.

AUGUST SIXTH

The Big Boys and Early Girls are plodding along, delivering modest quantities of better-than-store-bought fruit, but it's the two cherry tomato plants that have flourished. They have thrown their thin limbs clear over the deer fence, some of them taller than I am. The lath frame keeps them loosely corralled, though some of the runners, weighted with fruit, are growing sideways along the ground. These plants aren't merely successful, they're excited. The clusters of fruit are everywhere, as thick as grapes almost—hard green tiny apples, larger ones blushed fiery orange, pink pretenders, and scores of deep-crimson finished productions, swollen fatter than Ping-Pong balls, sagging the stems and dropping almost unbidden into my hands. As I explore the tangle on my knees, arms and face immersed in fragrant fuzziness, everything is red and green, Christmas in summer, and I know that the ones I pick make way for more tomorrow as the ripening tide of August floods full. A bowl of these little warm suns, a couple of cucumbers from the cucumber patch, then down to the cottage where olive oil and vinegar wait ready for their highest purpose, and whatever else we eat for dinner is only background.

13

It's strange to remember, we are so used to this abundance, that I didn't really trust those skinny plants I slipped from plastic cups and placed in the ground in April. Or I trusted them, I suppose, but I didn't trust myself to make them grow. Too much could go wrong: bugs, worms, blight, too much water, not enough water, wrong kind of soil, wrong kind of weather, and all the vaguer hazards that thronged my imagination. I thought my tomatoes would require a seasoned gardening expertise, and I didn't have it. I overrated my importance. The tomatoes, I can see now, have plenty of their own expertise. They have been around gardens a lot longer than I have, picking up pointers and remembering through generations, their intelligence trained to reliable brilliance by human selection.

And not only does the tomato know what to do, but the soil wants it done. My garden is the same ground as the field, where things grow on their own. I open a bit of the field to my suggestions, close it to the ideas of gophers and deer, and a garden happens. In fact, the entire field is a garden. The mustard it raises was scattered centuries ago by the padres, who wanted to connect their missions with a trail of golden light. The field likes the suggestion, and so repeats it year after year. And, of course, the field has its own ideas about what should grow, ideas borrowed from no human and unaltered by our lives. Its great oaks deepen imperceptibly into earth and air, all similar but each singular, each with a barrel trunk dividing into different configurations of crooked curving, and the limbs rebranching into finer and finer reticulations of twigs, as if the solid massy earth had fountained upward to turn itself into air.

Last night, walking in the field, I searched the jungle-gym tree with my flashlight. One of the fledgling great horned owls was there, but more than a fledgling now: its ear points were sharp, the lines of its face distinctly drawn, its throat patch white. It has come into its mature feathers, as the tomatoes and cucumbers of my garden have come into their full leaf and fruit.

AUGUST TWENTY-FIRST

Well, there's not much left. One plant behind the others half-escaped, but the rest are pretty well stripped —thickets of amputated stems, a disconsolate tomato still hanging here and there. I was careless and forgot my own lesson. Blurred the great distinction. Left the gate wide open, and my gentle neighbors have made me pay. As we slept last night they were here under a full moon fattening their ribby sides, the damn bandits. Cotton Mather was right: the wilderness is filled with evil, waiting for the slightest lapse of the innocent. Waiting patiently, with liquid brown eyes and twitching ears, with the delicate cloven hooves of the devil himself. Somewhere out in the field they're bedded down now, sleeping off their binge. I hope they're happy with themselves. I hope they have a bellyache for weeks.

AUGUST THIRTY-FIRST

Late tonight a wild medley of coyotes, close by in the field—frenzies of yips and barks, long trilling falsetto peals. We rarely hear them, never so close. As always, I imagine them burning, they give themselves so entirely to song. I slip out of the cottage, certain that this time I will penetrate their mystery. I will see what makes them sing. At the field's edge I click on my light. Sudden quiet. I see only the brief embers of their eyes, fading into night.

SEPTEMBER NINETEENTH

Bright blustery day, the oak limbs stirring, Wally's dusty blue eucalyptus swirling like seaweed in the pull of waves. The buckeye leaves have long shriveled and fallen, and now the oaks begin to let theirs go, to crunch underfoot along our trail. The first golden-crowned sparrows have arrived, with their sweetly plaintive song of three descending notes, and quail are everywhere—rustling nervously in the red poison oak, exploding out of thickets to cluck and twitter in the trees, and pecking their way up the field each evening, their silly topknots bobbing like feathered ornaments on antique hats.

Things are moving again. Breathing is a new pleasure. Wally and I rake leaves together, filled with energy and good talk. Two crows fly over the oaks, cawing their black speech, and high above the field a red-tailed hawk tilts in the wind. Then, at evening, the air falls still. A warming overnight, and Marilyn and I wake this morning smelling it before we see, the slanting scant gray motion of silent rain.

SEPTEMBER TWENTY-FIRST

I don't think I'll hear the owls again. Toward the end of August their juvenile rasps gave way to first attempts at the adult five-note call: *hoo hoo-hooo hooo hooo.* It came out a bit quavery and tentative in their unused voices, not the sure deep piping of the grown owls. And one of them couldn't quite finish the call—the first four *hoo*s came fluidly, though tremulous, but the final note kept slipping in his throat and coming out a strangled, high-pitched *squawk?* Earlier they had found their wings and feathers, now they were trying to find their voices. Then, a week ago, I surfaced out of sleep to hear the two of them piping back and forth. Their voices echoed through the emptiness of my half-conscious mind, back and forth, call and response and call again, each note and cadence whole, each delivered as it had to be. I haven't heard them since.

SEPTEMBER TWENTY-SECOND

Groping up to my shoulder in the scratchy stem-thicket, I locate the base of a vine and pull. The tomato plant's brittle, hollowed body almost leaps in my hand, leaving only a slight disturbance in the hardened ground. Over the fence with it, over the fence with all of

17

them. Deer can nose for the last half-ripe fruit, gleaning the few that they and I missed, and through the deer their seeds will go to the field. These plants have spoken long and well, and may again.

The cucumber vines too are yellowing, stiffening, some of their leaves already shriveled to dry corpses, but they are still producing fat yellow fruit, swelling on their sides like little pumpkins in the shade of the drying leaves. As if, having outgrown their early extravagance, their indiscriminate sprawling, they have now discovered their real work—the bearing of fruit—and go about it with the steadiness of maturity. They have arrived at their *metier,* and they pursue it.

I too have work to do, in my own kind of expression. In me as well, darkness would say something to the light. But the cucumbers are steadier than I am, and more productive. They have turned their entire being to their work; I do that only for brief intervals. Their vine-bodies are drying, beginning to disintegrate around the produce of their labor, and my body also is beginning to dry, to loosen, to accumulate aches and stiffnesses. It is not as old as the cucumber vines but getting older, and with fewer fruit to show. There is work to be done, there are meanings to make whole and ripe, and now—always now—is their season.

Pack Rat

IT BEGAN WITH faint slow stirrings above the dinner table where I sat writing. The sounds were soft as pencil rub, so scarcely audible they seemed born in my mind, some obscure rhythm of thought, an idea faintly scratching its way to awareness. Then it ran. It skittered loud across the ceiling tiles toward the kitchen, and I knew we had a rat.

In the two-room shack on an Oregon ranch where I used to live, I'd had a whole succession of rats. There was almost always one of them in residence with me, rambling down to the kitchen at night to gnaw at a pear or rip a loaf of bread to a scatter of shreds on the counter, then scampering around in the attic on rat business while I tried to sleep. My neighbors across the road had the answer: a live trap, an oblong wooden box with a drop-door held up by a network of sticks. The rat goes in for the bait, brushes the trigger stick, the door falls, and he's a trapped rat.

It was pack rats I was dealing with, so the baiting was easy. Anything would do—a bottle cap, a matchbook, a

19

wad of foil. I caught one rat with two nickels and a quarter from my pocket. Cheese or bread would have worked too, of course, but I liked the cleanliness of using non-food items. It was purely a business operation, the poor rodent done in not by bodily need but by his own sheer covetousness.

When I caught a rat I'd stick the trap in the back of my pickup, drive five miles up to Gerber Reservoir, and turn him loose. It was a fair shake, I think. Plenty of wild country up there where a wild rat ought to be able to live, but also, in the summer, plenty of fishermen camping in their motor homes—the fishermen who drove ceaselessly past my shack as weekends rolled around. If the rat needed human company, they could provide it. As soon as I got rid of one, of course, some kind of vacancy sign went up and another moved in.

I'd never had a close look at a pack rat, so the first one I trapped I wanted to see. I placed the trap mouth to mouth with a wire mesh cage, then tilted them together and shook him from one jail into the other. He sprang from side to side of the cage like a gymnast gone wild—frenzied, no doubt, by the blinding daylight he'd never been so lost in before. I was surprised how unrepulsive he looked. His black eyes bulged comically; the tail, nearly as long as his body, wasn't bare but furred with brown hair. His belly was white, and so were his feet. All in all, a pretty good-looking animal. He settled down when I draped my jacket over the cage, and when I turned him loose at Gerber he legged it straight to a rotting log and disappeared.

So I knew about rats, and next trip north to visit the ranch I borrowed the wooden box trap and brought it home. This rat wasn't getting into our kitchen, not into our rooms at all, but he was running around in the walls and ceiling enough to bother us at night, and occasionally he'd settle down to a long bout of gnawing—as if he were boring through the walls to join us, or chewing the electrical wires, as Marilyn imagined. It sounded like his passage to the world was in the kitchen area, so I set the trap in the crawl space underneath. In the morning, the drop-door was down. I lay with a flashlight and carefully cracked it. Nothing inside but the slice of bread and tea strainer I'd used for bait.

Then, as I started to reset the trap, I saw what I was up against. Oregon ranch rats were one thing; this Bay Area breed, it seemed, was something else entirely. Three notched sticks fit together to suspend the trap door, and one of them was gone. The smartass had not only sprung the trap from outside, he had left it inoperable.

I split a thin piece from a pine board and set to whittling, thinking of the first and, till now, smartest rat to have entered my life. Uncle Tom's home was a cabin on the Blue Ridge of Virginia that my parents bought as a weekend place around 1960. The cabin's hand-hewn beams went back to the early 1800s, and as far as anybody knew, Uncle

Tom did too. He was a bare-tailed rat, I think, and big—though any rat would have seemed big to me then. He kept a dignified distance, mostly, unless we left some food in the kitchen he couldn't resist. My mother thought he was fine. It was his place more than ours, she said. We were just weekenders.

But my father didn't like the idea of a rat in the place, so he set out to kill Uncle Tom. One weekend he brought enormous mousetraps, powerful enough to break a rat's neck. He baited them with cheese and found them undisturbed on Saturday morning, and Sunday morning, and next weekend when we returned. And so, to my mother's disgust, he bought poison—the kind in the little cardboard boxes you open and place under sinks and in closets where dogs can't get it. These too went untouched, for days and weeks. My father bought a different brand of poison. This time, during the week or two we were gone, Uncle Tom found a pair of my father's boxer shorts and left it draped over one of the poison boxes.

After that, my father resigned himself to live and let live, or seemed to. But eventually a friend of his brought a wire live trap to the cabin, and next morning Uncle Tom was in it. My father and his friend spent a long time deciding how to kill him. The mesh of the trap was too fine to shoot the .22 through, so they filled a washtub with water and together plunged the trap to the bottom and held it there, work gloves on their hands, their faces pale. I saw the rat dart and bump the cage in his frenzy, and then I didn't watch.

Not only the first night, but two of the next three as well, the rat of my present life springs my trap and hauls off parts of its workings. I'm getting good practice in whittling sticks, but I'm getting no rat. And so, for lack of a more sensible idea, I pry off a piece of the kitchen wall paneling where his noises seem to be focused, and there's his nest—a foot-and-a-half mound of shredded insulation giving off a sweetly urinous scent. *Things* are in and around this hill of rat domesticity: acorns, a wine cork, bits of foil and cardboard, two razor blades, a package of Stimu-Dents, a ballpoint pen cap—one of mine, I'm positive—a nub of yellow pencil, and two of my whittled sticks. It's an odd feeling staring at his life-heap, this between-walls home he has made, not in the cottage and not out. I haven't seen Stimu-Dents since I was a kid. How many rats have added to this nest? I feel vaguely guilty, as if I've violated a place I have no right to be. . . . But no, it's the other way around. I find the hole in the subfloor where he comes and goes—has gone, for now—and smugly nail a board over it.

For a few nights, peace. Then the scuttle of rat again, closer this time, in the wall by the bedroom doorway, which has no door, and in the ceiling just outside. He bustles intermittently for hours with his fine nocturnal energy, scrabbling down into the wall and after a while scrabbling up and across the ceiling, pausing briefly to gnaw now and then, as if suddenly remembering he should exercise his teeth. I'd rather be sleeping, but still, I hearken to him. He's on a roll, this rat. Sometimes I work that way myself, riding a nighttime wave from one piece of writing to another as each presents itself, finishing nothing but touching everything, everything fluid in my mind.

A few hard slaps on the ceiling quiet him; he makes whispery scratching sounds, then nothing. Back in bed in semi-sleep I try to imagine him, huddled silent in his own world separated from ours by an eighth-inch of wood veneer. What's in his mind? Is there anything, some dim meditation on what it means, those sudden booming shakes from below? What's it like to live in such tight spaces, such perfect dark. . . . I see him crouching, quiet, his muzzle faintly twitching, an aura of secret knowledge about him.

Sometime after we've fallen asleep he's rattling around again, so loud I think at first he's found a way inside, in the closet now, scratching underneath the bed. Occasionally he whaps his tail—it must be his tail, or maybe a foot—in a quick percussive drumroll. With ear plugs and a fan going for white noise, we eventually get some sleep. I can still hear him, of course. His scratching and rattling and gnawing are piercing sounds, and after a while I'm listening for them, fixated, measuring the silences between his flurries.

The next two nights are much the same, and I'm at a loss. I've tried the trap again, both under the cottage and on the roof, and now he just ignores it. Much too busy for it, to judge from what we hear. I've plugged a few cracks and holes I've found on the outside of the place, to no avail. Or have I trapped him in the walls? Is he going to die in there—running maniacally to the end—and stink the cottage from his secret crypt? But the pattern of his noises, those bursts of activity with silence between, says he's coming and going unimpeded.

Finally one morning I wake up with a decision already made. After teaching I drive to the hardware store for poison. We would give him our walls, but we won't give him our sleep.

To place the stuff where he's liable to find it, I have to take down one of the wood veneer ceiling panels. I work it carefully, trying to loosen the nails without splintering the veneer, and finally, as one edge drops loose in my hands, a shower of acorns rains on my head and clatters to the floor. So that's what he's been up to. Acorns have been dropping on the roof and all around the cottage for weeks; it's a good year, a bumper crop. Admiring their mahogany varnish, we've brought a few inside and placed them in a basket on the bookshelf. Now I've got a hundred of them on my floor. Doing my part in one of the odder seed dispersal systems in all of natural history, I gather the acorns and heave them out the door.

When I'm not actually lying awake in bed cussing him and jumping up to slap the ceiling, hoping not just to silence him but to give him a concussion, it's hard to hate this rat. He's gotten a lot of work done, and there's something very winning about his industry—his business so sensible, it turns out, and pursued with such innocent vigor. He's got a sense of humor, too. He keeps me in my place, but he does it with imagination and impishness. I leave the poison boxes in their bag and replace the ceiling panel. It wouldn't work anyway. This rat is not only crafty, he's well-fed.

New World rats and mice, it says in my Audubon guide, compose the largest family of mammals in North America—nineteen genera, seventy species, nested in every habitat in the land. Not surprising. If the greater clan is as canny and ambitious as our cottage mate, it's bound to prosper. Based on where we are, it seems our rat is probably a dusky-footed wood rat. Buff-brown, belly washed with tan. White toes. Omnivorous and nocturnal, like me. After mating, it says, the males live separately—so we likely have a husband, on the lam until the kids clear out. That's hopeful. Maybe he'll leave before long. But what were all those acorns for? The trading habit, my book says, is common to wood rats. They'll drop what they were carrying to pick up something else, especially something bright. No one knows why, but I understand it. You can make something good that way, dropping what you started with when something better flashes—collect enough flashes, and sometimes you've got a poem.

Our rodent-in-residence is collecting hard that night, restoring his stash. Now that we know what he's doing, the trail of his noises is clear. He drops down into the wall, then silence for a few minutes, sometimes half an hour. When he returns from acorn hunting he climbs the wall and skitters quickly through the ceiling. Sometimes— there's nothing else it could be—he drops the acorn he's been carrying and bowls it, or maybe bats it soccer-style, or noses it, somehow sends it rattling across the ceiling to its appointed place. And then he stops cold for ten seconds, a minute, three minutes. I have the surest sense he's baiting us, he's doing it on purpose, just *daring* us to slide off into sleep.

It's our house, I hear myself thinking. This rat has the run of the entire hillside, thickets and grass and intertwining oaks where he could ramble forever, and here he is, clattering in and out some rat-door I can't find like a happy speed freak, bowling acorns for his pleasure ten feet from where we lie not sleeping *in our own house.* I'm tired and mad enough to rip the ceiling down, acorns, insulation, the whole damn thing, except I know it wouldn't help. He knows my house better than I do. He'd dodge ahead along his secret passageways, laughing as I tore the place to shambles.

But how *will* we get rid of him? We joke about giving him the cottage and moving to a Palo Alto apartment. We joke, and after dinner the next evening I go out back and set up the tent. When we turn in we're comfortable there, under quilts on a thick foam pad, and it's wonderfully quiet, just a hint of wind in the Monterey pine. Exile could be worse. Maybe tomorrow night we'll sleep out in the field, and the next night over by the big eucalyptus where the red-shouldered hawk likes to perch, and then still farther, ranging wilder and wilder up the Santa Cruz hills. And our rat, meanwhile, will gnaw out of the walls and roam the cottage, forgetting his acorns as he grows soft and paunchy on our leftovers and bread . . .

Well—there's justice in it, says the rodent in my head. We don't own the cottage, after all. We didn't build it. We found it more or less by accident, as he did, and nested it with things, just like him. And *he* didn't come from far away, either—he was born on this hill, of parents born here the same. But never mind his lineage. What about his generosity? He's perfectly content to share the place, asking only for the inside of the walls. Why are *we* so intolerant?

Because it's our house, damn it. He may have a valid biotic claim, and he may have won the cottage for the night, but I have a bigger brain, and I'm not done yet. I like sleeping outdoors, but no rat is going to *make* me sleep outdoors. We're not just weekenders, we *live* here. And if I can find his secret door, he won't.

It has to be under the bedroom wall. And so I spend the next morning prying off sheets of paneling and peering among studs and electric wires with a flashlight. There's a small opening through the subfloor next to the doorway, but it's more a crack than a hole. I can't believe a beast as loud as our friend could fit through that, so I go on dismantling to the end of the wall. The desiccated corpse of a mouse rests on a two-by-four ledge, but no hole. It has to be the crack by the door. I remember hearing, I think, they can supple themselves to pass through tight places. I nail down a plug and put the wall back together, taping instead of nailing the panel in front of the plugged hole. I don't know what's going to happen, but *something* is, whether I've blocked him in or blocked him out.

I'm hoping out, but of course he's in. In bed we hear him moving around the ceiling at half-speed, probably just waking up, and when he drops down into the wall for his first journey out I'm ready. I pull the taped panel just far enough from the framing to slip in a piece of two-by-four I've cut to fit tight between the two studs. I tape up the panel and he's a trapped rat, plugged below and now above. He knows it, too, because he's very quiet the rest of the night.

There's no time to deal with him in the morning, but I'm in no hurry. He's not going anywhere. My day passes in an aura of satisfied accomplishment. That evening, though, when Marilyn and I are home from work, I'm struck with doubt. This is the rat, after all, who has foiled and ridiculed my every attempt to catch him. And it's awfully quiet in that wall. I crack open the top of the taped panel and scan the bottom of the cell, using a flashlight and a small mirror. He's there, all right, nosed into a corner. But he looks unbelievably small—more of a mouse than a rat. A trick of the mirror, I suppose.

After all that's happened, I'm glad we've caught him alive. He's been a worthy adversary. It will be a pleasure to release him—many many miles away—to assemble his new nest and get on with his life. The trouble is, though, we haven't really caught him. He's trapped in his cell of wall, but how do we get him out of there? A fishing net might do the trick, if I had one, but I don't. Rummaging in a crowded closet, I find a small cardboard box, a little larger than rat-size. The best idea I can come up with is to hold it upside down and lower it over him from above. Marilyn is doubtful, but it's time to act. It's time to get him gone.

As things stand now he's out of my reach, so I put on my work gloves and saw across the taped panel three feet above the floor. Then, as Marilyn stands behind me holding a sheet outstretched—our safety containment—I take off the top section and slowly lower the box. The rat looks a lot bigger and the box a lot punier as it gets closer to him, but now I'm committed. He squirms a little deeper into the corner. He's a caught rat, I'm thinking, when just as the box is about to cover him he explodes up my arm, launches from my shoulder past Marilyn's face, and scuttles into the bedroom and under the bed.

Marilyn is making guttural noises. I am standing quietly like the fool I am, who has not only failed to catch a cornered rat but personally presented him a convenient pathway into our house. The bed, a pine platform on cinder blocks, has lots of things under it—suitcases, pillows, a box of photos, bags of this and that. He's buried somewhere in that nest-clutter, probably feeling a lot safer than he did a minute ago. I get the wok cover from the kitchen, and with that in my left hand, hoping for another chance, I start removing what's there, tapping each item and gingerly dragging it out. He shoots out of the empty blue duffel just as I touch it. I clap down the cover too late—of course I'm too late—and he's under the dresser in the corner of the room.

Shining the flashlight along the wall, I can see him crouching, but I can't get to him. Marilyn and I look at each other. "You'd better ask Wally for his pellet gun," I tell her.

I stand in the doorway, in case the rat decides to run, but he's not going anywhere. He's crowding himself into the corner, trying his best to disappear. Everything in him wants to go back to the comfortable close-quartered darkness he knows. But he's trapped for good now, he's loose where he didn't want to be and where we can't allow him to stay. He's caught on the wrong side of our walls, too fast and too smart for us in our blundering ways to save him.

Marilyn returns with Wally, Wally with the gun, and

we arrange ourselves for the finish. Wally kneels in the doorway with my pry bar in his hand, Marilyn stands behind him with the sheet, but of course the rat stays put. He squirms as my first shot hits him in the side. I don't know if the second hits him at all. The third shot kills him.

Walking into the field with his body in a plastic bag, though he's probably cleaner than I am, I tell myself it had to be done. I tried harder than most people would have to catch him alive. He was driving us crazy, and now at least we'll have our sleep back. It's all true, but I've never felt more thoroughly defeated. I think of all the times I've hiked the mountains or scrambled up desert canyons hoping for a glimpse, or if not a glimpse just a track or scat, some brief witness of a life not human or touched by humans. A creature as wild and intelligent and worthy as any in those far places comes to where we live, gets tangled in our sensibilities, and the best I can do is what Americans have always done. Necessarily, as any reasonable householder would, I trained my vision through the sights of a gun.

But it's not just the rat. He had to go, and remorseful as I now feel, there were many nights I would have gladly murdered him. The field is absolutely still tonight, no movement in the oaks or dry grasses. I can hear the whispered background surge of cars on I-280. Down the hill, something rustles. We still see animals here. A few deer, who browse the grass when it's green and stay close to our watered oasis in the summer drought. And raccoons, who are so adaptable they thrive in city alleys. Once in a while a coyote, the master survivor. But thirty and forty years ago, Wally says, when his was the only house for half a mile, this place teemed with animals. He and Mary saw amazing things. A pair of gray foxes would groom themselves on the porch of his study, six feet from where he watched. Once a red-tail flew across the patio wrestling with a gopher snake, nearly crashing at their feet. Then bulldozers carved the hills, new homes kept rising along new roads, the animals slipped away. We see remnants now. And when this field goes to houses, as it will before long, the remnants too will disappear.

A jet rumbles over toward San Francisco Airport. The night sky is never still around here. A few stars are out, washed pale as they always are by the diffused radiance of the greater Peninsula, ranging away to the north in a twinkling swath from where I stand. And closer, circling almost all around the field, the lights of neighboring homes shine steadily—porch lights, street lights, security floodlamps, lit windows, a constellation of human residence, rooms where people eat and speak and have their lives, where children grow. We need those rooms. We need the walls we put around us. But dropping the pack rat in the field, I wish we knew some other way of building them, I wish we could live in our human house without sweeping it so clean of other lives.

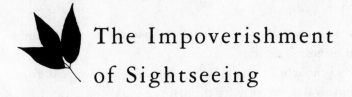

The Impoverishment
of Sightseeing

WHEN I WAS a boy my family had a week-
end cabin on the Blue Ridge of northern Virginia, and it
was on one of my hikes in the woods nearby that I experienced a new standard of fear. I was walking alone on a
sunny day when I came to a slope of small gray boulders,
bare of vegetation. I had skirted this boulder patch on
previous rambles, and wondered about it, and now I decided to cross it. As I hopped from rock to rock, a quick
buzz from below froze me. *Cicada,* I thought hopefully, but
I knew what it was. I jumped to another rock and another
buzz sounded, then another. The whole bright strew of
boulders seemed to be buzzing around me, beneath me, and
one more step, I was sure, would bring lightning fangs. I
tried to quiet my tremoring legs, to stand as still and light
and thin as it was possible to stand. I'm sure I prayed—
prayer was my habit in those days when things weren't
going well. I stood for probably half an hour, long after the
buzzes had stopped. Finally I boosted my courage, stepped
to the very crown of the next rock, and accompanied by

sporadic buzzes, danced out of the boulder field with the nimbleness of dread.

I thought of that childhood ordeal when I visited Yosemite Valley recently for the first time in over a decade. In my mid-twenties I knew the Valley as a rock climber of high enthusiasm and modest ability. Now, at thirty-seven, I was returning with my wife and mother, neither of whom had seen Yosemite before. I wanted to show them the exhilarating playground I had known. Because my mother wasn't a strong walker, we decided to take our first long look from one of those buses that loop around the Valley floor. With its solid bank of windows curving up over our heads, we thought the bus would give us many good views, and it did. But how disappointing those views were, how unaccountably dull. The familiar rock faces all were there, as sheer and massive as ever, but *merely* there. As the bus trundled along they paraded through the frame of my window, one after another, as I tried hard to feel excited.

What I saw was dull, I realized after a while, because I was walking the boulder field without the snakes. The places that had once been alive to me, imbued with my zeal and fears, now were reduced to plain visual images, seen for the sake of seeing, *scenes* in the bus window. My wife and mother, viewing Glacier Point and Half Dome for the first time, were more satisfied with what they saw. But I sensed no real enthusiasm from them as the sunny granite shifted in our window view, nor from the other passengers, most of whom were clearly new to the Valley. "Look at that," the man in front of us kept murmuring, but listlessly, like a recorded message. "Isn't that a sight. Isn't that a sight."

When I climbed those rocks—only a few hundred feet up most of them—they were not sights but presences. As I focused on cracks and tiny nubbins in front of my face, bright granite expanse was always flaring in the periphery of my vision—all the more vivid, all the more present, for being only obliquely seen. And just as vivid and present was what I couldn't yet see, the challenges that lay hidden where the route disappeared above an overhang or around a corner. It was that perpetual unknown that buzzed me with scary excitement, like rattlesnakes hidden beneath boulders —that was what I climbed after, more beautiful than anything I saw with my eyes.

As I looked out from a belay ledge after a hard pitch, the far Valley wall wavered and swam with squiggly spots, nothing solid about it, then settled in my vision not merely to stone but to an embodiment of spirit. Having made a pitch I wasn't sure I could make, I was suffused with a sense of body and mind doing exactly what they were meant to do, blended perfectly in their most rightful act. And what was that arched and pinnacled rising of granite I gazed at, shining through a gulf of air, but the world's own most perfect and rightful act?

One July weekend my partner and I tried the Chouinard-Herbert route on Sentinel Rock, a 1,700-foot face normally done in two days. Mid-morning on the second day, after a bivouac on a ledge, we killed our last bottle of water—we had badly miscalculated our need—and climbed ahead into the ninety-degree afternoon. We became so weak we couldn't finish the climb by dark, though we had reached the easy ledges near the top. We spent another night, sleeping like stones as the brightest colors I have ever seen flamed through my dreams. In the morning we made our way to the top, there to find an enormous orange-barked ponderosa pine, standing alone. It seemed to glow from within, a tree but more than a tree, an emblem of being itself. And the stream we finally came to, after what seemed hours of stumbling descent down the dry gully behind Sentinel, was no ordinary stream with a fringe of plants—how *green* those plants were—but the very Garden itself. We knelt there, feeling the icy glow of water inside us with our booming and skittering hearts.

Rock climbing and mountaineering are unnecessary, artificial activities, invented by a privileged leisure class. Yet the act of climbing can yield an engagement with the natural world that is anything but artificial. That, I believe, is the reason it arose among the European well-to-do of the nineteenth century—it answered a need for reconnection to the wild nature from which they had so successfully separated themselves. Other kinds of outdoor activities answer the same need for many who pursue them—backpacking, birding, hunting, fishing, white-water rafting. They offer in common the opportunity to be actively involved with nature instead of passively receiving it. Climbers and fishermen may not be at one with nature, but they are immersed in it, interact with it, and in that sense they are part of their surroundings. They experience a sense of place in nature, or at least that experience is potentially available to them. Those who come to sightsee, on the other hand, are not part of the place they look at. They are observers, subjects seeking an object, passing through.

I don't mean that the population can be divided into two groups, the doers and the lookers. I am both, at different times. All of us at various moments are the man on the bus gazing out and murmuring, "Isn't that a sight." Nor do I believe that that man was completely disconnected from what he saw; he was impressed, perhaps even moved, by the spectacle of Yosemite's walls. But he wasn't moved in any way that energized him much, that evoked any sign of elation or fear or awe. Like me at the time, he wasn't in the *presence* of those soaring faces. And as I watched him and others clicking photographs later, I couldn't help thinking that by recording what they saw they were trying to verify that it was real, and that they were actually there.

I've experienced that odd feeling myself. The first time I saw the Tetons I was a teenager sightseeing with my family. We sat at an outdoor chuckwagon breakfast place, eating pancakes and staring at the most dramatic mountains

I had ever seen, so dramatic my eyes didn't quite believe them. They seemed to have no depth, hardly any substance —I kept thinking they looked like cut-outs someone had propped up on the other side of the lake. Part of my trouble, I'm sure, was due to the fact that an eastern kid was seeing his first western mountains. But I think there was more. I was expecting to experience those mountains, to perceive their full reality, simply by looking at them from a distance. They seemed to lack substance because I was reducing them to an image on the screen of my vision.

I suspect that television—I used to watch a lot of it— had much to do with my perception of the Tetons, as I suspect it has much to do with the way many of us experience the natural world. Television viewers give up the active movements of awareness—glancing around, comparing, looking long or only briefly—to the autocratic screen, reducing themselves to mere absorbers of the presented image. All of us who spend much time in such a mode of consciousness will necessarily transfer it to other areas of experience. When we go into nature, we will expect the things we see to reveal themselves, to tender their full value, merely by lying in our field of vision. And to the extent that nature seems static and dramatically blank compared to TV entertainment, it is likely to seem disappointing, lifeless, and unreal.

Even nature documentaries, despite their educational value, may tend ultimately to diminish the viewer's engagement with nature rather than enhance it. Those who are used to such programs are likely to find real nature—subliminally, at least—disorderly and dull, because its images aren't preselected for visual impact and framed within a screen. Shows about nature may come to seem more real than nature itself. For millions of Americans, it may be that the viewing of such programs, and of television in general, is substantially replacing direct experience of the wild natural world. When an old-growth forest is delivered to the living room, some viewers will want to go there. But far more, I think, will feel they have already been.

What that majority will miss, of course, is the unframed sensory texture of the thing itself—the scale of the trees, the pervasive stillness and the filtered ambient light, the dark smells of the forest floor, the feel of moss under their feet. They will miss the varying rhythms of their walking and the unconstrained movements of awareness in such a place. They will miss the primordial alertness that comes in the presence of trees, shadows, and small forest sounds, of wildlife seen and unseen. Consuming the image rather than the thing, they will have walked the boulder field not only without the snakes but without the boulders, and without themselves.

But more is at stake than the quality of our perception. Reducing nature to a collection of visual objects seen on television, or even firsthand, is not only impoverishing to us, but dangerous to the land as well. Nature-as-sight affords a purely aesthetic appeal to the seer, a pleasing pattern of form and color—what we generically call "natural beauty." There is nothing wrong with aesthetic appreciation, and it can lead to other ways of valuing nature, but it seems to me a very fragile basis for preserving what relatively wild, undisturbed lands we have left. When push comes to shove, as the settlement of North America has made clear, aesthetic values have a way of toppling in the practical path of progress. Tall-grass prairie was beautiful to the Ohio Valley settlers, but they plowed it under. The passenger pigeon was beautiful to the hunters who shot it down. Even timber executives see beauty in old-growth Douglas fir, but its beauty doesn't stop them from reducing it to clearcuts.

Appreciation of nature in our society takes two forms above all others. The prevailing form, the cult of utility, shapes and perpetuates our sense of land as something from which to extract uses and materials. The other, the cult of beauty, values land for its own sake, but chiefly for its visual appearance. The cult of beauty has had important positive consequences—most of our national and state parks were set aside because of their scenic splendor—but it also works hand-in-hand with the cult of utility. Our working assumption as a people has been that except for a scattering of parks and designated wilderness areas, many of them in alpine regions difficult of commercial access anyway, all other land is subject to utility first and other considerations second.

On public lands, the much-voiced concept of multiple-use says that scenery and recreation are equal in importance to the land's utilitarian value; but in practice, multiple-use in our national forests means logging first and other uses where logging permits. And in the desert West, which even in the eyes of many nature lovers still lies outside the category of the beautiful, mining, oil and gas drilling, and the wholesale stripping of forest to create range for cows all proceed with practically no restraint.

When those who oppose such "improvements" invoke in its defense only (or mainly) the land's beauty, they are dismissed as sentimental and unrealistic. And there is a certain justice in the dismissal, because at bottom the cult of beauty shares with the cult of utility the same flaw: it views nature as an object separate from the human subject. The timber or mineral executive reduces nature to a commodity, something to be taken out. The tourist seeking scenic beauty reduces nature to pleasing images, enjoyed and taken home on film. Neither recognizes nature as a living system of which our human lives are part, on which our lives and all lives depend, and which places strict limits upon us even as it sustains us.

That is an ecological view, and though most of us have some familiarity with the ideas of ecology, ecology remains *only* ideas, abstract and forceless in our lives, so long as we perceive nature merely as a collection of objects, however lovely. It takes not just looking at nature but getting into

43

it—into some of its unloveliness as well as its splendor—
for ideas to begin to bear the fruit of understanding. The
rattlesnakes beneath the boulders instructed me, in a way
no book could have, that the natural world did not exist
entirely for my comfort and pleasure; indeed, that it did
not particularly care whether my small human life continued to exist at all. Being terribly thirsty on Sentinel Rock
helped me understand in my body what my mind already
knew, or thought it knew—how moisture both makes life
possible and sets unequivocal limits on where it can exist.
And once I had spent some time in old-growth forests, the
profusion of dead trees that had daunted me at first began
to elicit an appreciation of how death and life dance to a
single music, how a healthy natural community carefully
conserves and recycles its living wealth, and so sustains
itself through time.

Such perceptions, in their rudimentary way, point toward an ecological understanding of the natural world.
Clearly, to fully realize this understanding, we as a people
need to follow the lead of the ecological sciences and learn
to live by the principles they discover. We need to heal the
injuries we have caused in the biosphere. But even as we
scientifically study the inner workings of nature and the
ways we have disrupted it, we also need to experience it
again, to apprehend it in its fullness. As Edward Abbey
told us many times, we can't experience the outdoors
through a car window. We must take the time to enter the

44

natural world, to engage it, not just to run our eyes along its surfaces but to place ourselves among its things and weathers—to let it exert, at least for intervals in our lives, the ancient influences that once surrounded and formed us.

Enough time under those influences can teach us to use our eyes actively again, as something more than receptacles. They seek a route through trees, across a creek, over a ridge, working in concert with body and mind. They follow the darts and veers of a hummingbird, a lizard skimming across stones, the quick glint of a trout. Things much smaller than El Capitan or the Tetons, things easy to miss, begin to reveal themselves—tiny white flowers of saxifrage, the quarter-sized, web-lined shaft of a tarantula's den, a six-inch screech owl flicking limb to limb in the dusk.

And when later in the evening the owl sounds its soft, tremulous call, and small snaps and rustlings reveal the presence of other lives, the eyes have reached their proper limit. The sense we rely on above all others can never completely know the natural world, for nature's being is only partly what it shows. Its greater part, and greater beauty, is always past what human eyes can understand. When I started hiking desert canyons a few years ago, I kept hearing the song of a bird I couldn't see, a long descending series of sharply whistled notes. It was a canyon wren, I learned from the books, but what I learned from the bird was more important. It sang as I woke up, as brilliant sun spread down the great red walls, and it sang as I started farther up the twisting canyon, sloshing through pools and scrambling up dry water chutes, higher and deeper into the carving of time. And what I remember most vividly from those early hikes is no particular thing I saw, no one fern grotto or sandstone spire, no cottonwood or cactus' garden. I remember a bird I couldn't see that called from around the next bend, from over the brink of a dry waterfall where the upper walls held the blaze of sky, where even as it steadily opened itself to sight, the canyon receded further and further into the depth of its mystery.

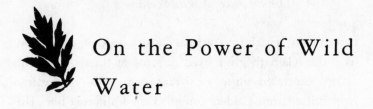

On the Power of Wild Water

By such a river it is impossible to believe that one will ever be tired or old. Every sense applauds it. Taste it, feel its chill on the teeth: it is purity absolute. Watch its racing current, its steady renewal of force: it is transient and eternal. And listen again to its sounds: get far enough away so that the noise of falling tons of water does not stun the ears, and hear how much is going on underneath—a whole symphony of smaller sounds, hiss and splash and gurgle, the small talk of side channels, the whisper of blown and scattered spray gathering itself and beginning to flow again, secret and irresistible, among the wet rocks.

—Wallace Stegner

THE KLAMATH RIVER begins its journey in south-central Oregon, flowing out of a shallow ancient lake that lies just east of the Cascade Range, where the fir and pine forest of the mountains gives way to the sage and juniper steppeland of the interior. The river runs southwesterly, bisecting the Cascades in a wide canyon on its way into California and on for two hundred miles to the sea. In that canyon, which the river has cut to a depth of a thousand feet, the Klamath gives itself to some of the most violent and concentrated white-water rapids in the West. For five river miles, from Caldera Rapid to the California line, the river is all waves and boulders and relentless roar, dropping as steeply as seventy-seven feet per mile before easing into a quiet slide and the broad slackwater of Copco Dam.

Along with osprey, beaver, and black-tailed deer, human beings have lived and camped in the Klamath River Canyon for thousands of years. Ancestors of the Klamath and Shasta Indians are buried there. The Shasta received their first medicine power there. People of both tribes hold the river and canyon sacred, returning there for spirit quests, healing rituals, and other ceremonies of their religious life, as well as for hunting and fishing. European-Americans have known the upper Klamath for less than a century and a half. A few ranchers pioneered the area, a stagecoach road went through, logs were chuted into the river and floated to the Klamathon mill. The twentieth century brought heavier settlement to the surrounding region, and with people and their burgeoning needs came dams to extract the river's power. The upper Klamath has been dammed four times, above and below the canyon, leaving only twenty miles of free-flowing stream.

In the early 1980s, the mayor and council of Klamath Falls, Oregon, announced plans for a new dam that would tap the energy of the canyon itself. By selling electricity into the Northwest power grid, the civic leaders hoped to create an annual income of three to ten million dollars for economic development in the area. Opposition to the Salt Caves Dam came immediately from white-water rafters, fishermen, environmentalists, and Indians, and the Federal Energy Regulatory Commission suggested an alternate proposal—instead of a dam, an eight-mile pipe would divert part of the river to a powerhouse downstream. Opponents argue that a diversion would damage the river almost as badly as a dam, and the question of whether to build the Salt Caves hydroelectric project is now inching toward resolution in the slow machinery of state and federal regulatory agencies. It will finally be decided, very likely, in the courts.

The fate of the project, and the fate of the last wild stretch of the upper Klamath River, will be determined largely on the basis of such factors as water temperature, dissolved oxygen content, stream turbidity, and a host of other technical considerations. These criteria are ways of measuring the river's health, and it's right that they be given substantial weight. But I have little command of, and little interest in, these data now being presented, studied, revised, and wrangled over in government offices and hearing rooms, and I believe there are other considerations of equal importance. I used to live in the Klamath Falls area, I have rafted the Klamath River, and I am against any dam or diversion. I base my position on nothing measurable by instruments, nothing spoken in the language of science. There are two voices I've been listening to, and I find them sufficient: the sound of wild water, and the words of a man who never saw either the Klamath River or the twentieth century.

In 1837, addressing his graduating class at Harvard, Henry David Thoreau took a position on the value of nature: "This curious world which we inhabit is more wonderful than it is convenient, more beautiful than it is useful—it is more to be admired and enjoyed then, than used."

Admired and enjoyed. The original sense of "admire" is to marvel at, to experience wonder. Wonder and joy, says Thoreau, are higher goods than any material use we can extract from nature. But Thoreau himself, even while holed up at Walden Pond to test his skill at wanting but little, used nature in addition to admiring and enjoying it. He broke the native grasses to plant his beans. He bought lumber to build his cabin—$8.03½ worth, he tells us. He bought paper to write on, books to keep him company. He delighted and found poetry in the knowledgeable uses of nature he observed in his neighbors, the farmer Minott, the fisherman Goodwin.

Yet I see no inconsistency between the way Thoreau lived at Walden and what he said at Harvard. He didn't say that nature was not to be used. He said that it was more to be admired and enjoyed than used, that use was not the highest good it offered. In the middle of the nineteenth century, Thoreau was seeing those values of use and enjoyment begin to clash. He saw the great white pines falling in Concord, saw the oak forest cleared and the soil used up in crops and given over to scrub. He watched and worried about a quickening procession of technology—railroad, telegraph, all the inventions and extensions of inventions that were opening the land to exploitation and inflating the American mind with a dangerously self-serving ethic: that whatever we *could* do with our machines and ingenuity, we *should* do. Thoreau was witnessing the rise of the cult of Progress, American-style, in whose enthusiastic view the abundance of the New World had been created solely for man's convenience and gain. In the words of Thomas Ewbank, a prosperous manufacturer of metallic tubing for the new technology, nature was a "complete machine-shop" to which "the Great Engineer" had "called in man to take possession and go to work."

It was this attitude that Thoreau opposed, not the wisely restrained use of wild nature that is compatible with its integrity and our sense of wonder and joy. When he died in 1862 he had probably seen enough to know that wise use was not going to prevail in North America. He did not specifically foresee the strip mining of the Appalachians and the extinction of the passenger pigeon and the muddying of the Mississippi with millions and millions of tons of the finest topsoil in the world. He did not know that by the 1880s sixty million buffalo would be nothing but bones and mounds of meat rotting on the plains, the hides and tongues stripped for sale. He had heard of the redwoods but never saw how big they were, never imagined the crosscuts slicing through twenty feet of trunk, the workmen standing, hands on hips, on the stumps of trees three thousand years old. Surely he never imagined the western copper pits, any one of which could swallow a thousand Walden Ponds, or the miles and miles of clearcuts spreading in the Cascades and Sierra Nevada, or the southwestern grasslands reduced by livestock to sand and sage. He didn't see these things, but he saw very clearly the shortsightedness and greed that would cause them.

Thoreau was a New Englander. Mount Katahdin in Maine was a big mountain to him, its upper reaches as alien and disconcerting as a mountain on the moon. The rivers he floated were the Concord and Merrimack, quiet waters with few riffles and rapids. He chose the stillness of a lake for his retreat: it reflected his spirit best, its depths spoke to his own. He was less moved by nature's raw power than by her small secrets, the symbols she perennially urged to his awareness, her mysterious benevolence through which, in his words, "I go and come with a strange liberty, a part of herself."

The crashing waters of the Klamath River Canyon probably would have made the man uneasy. I doubt you could have dragged him into a raft. Even so, I think I know how he would have felt about damming or diverting such a river. I think he would have responded just as he did to the forest of stumps and slash he once happened upon in the Maine woods. He wrote, turning his anger into a cutting clarity of phrase:

> The pine is no more lumber than man is, and to be made into boards and houses is no more its true and highest use than the truest use of a man is to be cut down and made into manure.

Is it the true and highest use of a river, Thoreau might have asked, to be diverted into electrical power? I can hear him saying: A river is not what it can be made to produce. A river is a natural act. Its true and highest purpose is to continue to be itself.

I imagine Thoreau turning the word "power" in his serious whimsical mind. What use do you make of your own power? I can hear him asking. Do you make of yourself a better person? Do you live with full power of consciousness? If it is power you wish from the river, then go to the river. Discover the power it holds for the rafters who give themselves to its currents. Find for yourself the power that draws the fishermen there, and the walkers, the watchers of animals, the couples, the solitary idlers. If it is power you wish, the river *is* power—a power less of use, a power more of wonder and of joy.

Four hundred miles from the Klamath River Canyon,

outside the main library of Stanford University, there is a fountain, a giant red ring that jets water downward to a pool. On sunny days, students gather on the grass nearby. They read, they talk, they look at one another, they sleep. They come to the fountain to do those things because the aura of watersound surrounds them there, the steady rushing, the song that smooths the sharp edges of nervousness and fear. In the deeps of the mind we know that song, we knew it before we first heard it, we've known it for all the eons of our coming of age on Earth. "It seems to flow through my very bones," writes Thoreau of a brook that falls into Fair Haven Pond. "What is it I hear but the pure waterfalls within me, in the circulation of my blood, the streams that fall into my heart?"

That fountain at Stanford represents to me all the glistening, trickling, gurgling, streaming, surging, roaring, falling, thundering waters of the world. In its subdued and steady way it stands for the tons of river crashing right now through the Klamath River Canyon and the Grand Canyon of the Colorado and every other gorge and valley across the continent where water has not been silenced by man. That fountain reminds me, whenever I walk in the reach of its sound, that the wild remnants of those once wholly wild streams must continue to flow as freely as they can, as freely as they flowed for millions of years before white man or Indian came close enough to hear.

The Klamath, like all American rivers, has been used

and misused. The civic leaders of Klamath Falls have argued
that because four dams exist, because the river is no longer
completely wild, another dam or diversion won't matter. In
Thoreau's time one of the rationalizations for the consumption of nature was its seeming boundlessness—what harm
could humans do to that immense vitality by taking what
they wanted? Now, as we approach the end of our original
inheritance, the argument goes that because nature isn't
natural anymore it might as well be completely harnessed
to human uses. In Thoreau's woods at Walden Pond that
logic has led to a highway, a landfill, and a trailer park. A
condominium project was barely defeated, and now an office
park is planned by a developer who claims priority for what
he calls "the built environment." On the upper Klamath
River the same logic has led to a built environment of four
dams enclosing one last length of wild water where nature
is more wonderful and enjoyable than useful.

But enjoyment can be had in other places, the civic
leaders have argued. To compensate for lost recreation on
the river, their original proposal included the development
of a ski resort on a nearby mountain. That view of nature,
in which landforms are reduced to counters on a bargaining
table, is exactly the view of Thomas Ewbank, the man who
perceived the natural world as a convenient assembly of
parts for human tinkering. Such a view sees opposites as the
same: the development of a wild mountain into a recreational resort is seen as equivalent to the enjoyment of an

undeveloped stretch of wild river. Among the followers of the cult of usefulness that governs our relations with nature, enjoyment itself has been subsumed as one more form of exploitation.

The purpose of the Salt Caves hydroelectric project is to make money for economic development in the region of Klamath Falls. The electricity it would produce is not presently needed in the area. But even if there were a need, it ought to be asked why the river should be required to fill that need. And it ought to be asked what we will do when there is no more dammable or divertable water and our appetite for energy, spurred and enlarged by the existing dams, still wants more. The boosters speak enthusiastically of the economic growth the project will generate, as if that were the answer to everything, and as if it had no cost beyond construction of the project itself. It has a cost. Economic growth means more human beings and greater human demands that nature will be made to pay.

For four hundred years we have burdened the North American continent with our ingenious greed. It is time, belatedly, to stop taxing those bits of wild nature we still have and to begin taxing our imaginations for a wiser, friendlier, and sustainable way of being. The power of free-running water, like the silent power of old-growth forest and the spacious power of desert, is not a commodity but a life. In the Klamath River Canyon, that life is at risk, its fate probably to be decided by the estimated effects of a one or two degree change in water temperature. We will be a saner society when such decisions don't depend on technical considerations alone. We will be a saner society when the issue under discussion in hearing rooms and agency offices around this country is not a proposal to build a new dam or diversion, but a proposal to dismantle an old one. And we will be a saner society when we remember the free and boisterous power of wild water for what it is—the song that sings its way through stone, more ancient and as filled with truth as any utterance of man, an original voice of Earth that celebrates, in its ceaseless fluid tongue, the same unfolding mystery that made us.

Place of Wild Beasts

"WILDERNESS," IN ITS Old English roots, means something like "wild beast place." On a recent backpacking trip in Oregon's Mount Jefferson Wilderness, I encountered two kinds of beast. The campsites in the broad and beautiful meadow of Jefferson Park were thronged with squirrels. And the squirrels were gorging themselves on bits of bread and oatmeal dropped by the other kind of beast, which also thronged the campsites, and the rest of the meadow as well. Both were clearly enjoying themselves—squirrels busy with their free meal, humans feasting on mountain scenery in the congenial clear warmth of early October. Neither acted particularly wild, and aside from a few late-season bugs and a bird or two, no other beast was in evidence.

When the Pilgrims made landfall at Cape Cod on a wintry November day in 1620, they stared at a wilderness such as the word was meant to describe. "Besides what could they see," William Bradford would write in *Of Plymouth Plantation*, "but a hideous and desolate wilderness, full of wild beasts, and wild men—and what multitudes there might be of them they knew not. . . ." The Pilgrims didn't cross the Atlantic to admire nature, of course. They came to make a home, and making a home required them to brave and subdue real dangers. Some of the wildness they faced, however, they brought with them. When Cotton Mather looked at a bird, he saw nothing innocent or beautiful, but a sinister enemy: "The *Birds of prey* (and indeed the *Devils* most literally in the shape of great *Birds!*) are flying about." Even the weather could be perceived as a conspiracy against the saints. "Once more," wrote Mather, "why may not *Storms* be reckoned among those *Woes* with which the Devil does disturb us?"

Mather's theologically freighted view, of course, wasn't the only attitude that the first settlers projected on the New World. To others it was an infinite source of useful commodities, a bonanza whose potential was whatever human ingenuity and human gumption could make of it. Where Mather saw Devils, many colonial Americans saw pounds and shillings. Thomas Morton, founder of the Merrymount community in Massachusetts and first of a long and undistinguished lineage of New World boosters, cheerfully looked at the land and declared it "Nature's Masterpeece: Her cheifest Magazine of all, where lives her store." And Morton lit upon another, more vivid metaphor for the teeming American wilderness, one that lifted him to awkward heights of poetry:

Place of Wild Beasts

Like a faire virgin, longing to be sped,
And meete her lover in a Nuptiall bed,
Deck'd in rich ornaments t' advaunce her state
And excellence, being most fortunate,
When most enjoyed . . .

O fortunate land, so long and thoroughly enjoyed. Morton was talking, of course, in his genial way, about rape. And rape it would be, as the settlers' need to make a living blended with Puritan paranoia and with sheer avarice in the resource-stripping mania of Manifest Destiny. The rout of North America's life and land proceeded with such vigor and efficiency that voices of protest rose as early as the eighteenth century, then crescendoed in the nineteenth as Americans developed a Romantic taste for the wild sublime. "We need the tonic of wildness," wrote Thoreau. "At the same time that we are earnest to explore and learn all things, we require that all things be mysterious and unexplorable, that land and sea be infinitely wild. . . ." John Muir found the workings of nature not devilish but divine, and the modern conservation movement that followed in his wake eventually succeeded in codifying wilderness preservation into American law. Thus was the Puritan position officially reversed. In Bradford's and Mather's world, man needed protection from wilderness. Congress in 1964 decreed that wilderness needs protection from man.

Unfortunately, there isn't a great deal left to protect.

61

The Wilderness Act, without question, is a milestone law
—along with the Endangered Species Act, it is the boldest
and most intelligent thing our society has done in regard to
our relationship with wild nature. But aside from the fact
of its existence, the most striking feature of the National
Wilderness Preservation System is its diminutive size. A
map issued by the Wilderness Society to commemorate the
twenty-fifth anniversary of the act shows a sprinkling of
tiny pieces of protected land in the Ozarks, the Appalachians, New England, and the Lake Superior country. Only
three tracts of any considerable size lie east of the Rockies
—Okefenokee, the Everglades, and the Boundary Waters
Canoe Area. In the western states, larger splotches are more
numerous, especially in Idaho, western Montana, and
northwestern Wyoming. Smaller patches are scattered down
the spines of the Rockies and the Cascade-Sierra, and some
bits and pieces appear in the southwestern deserts and the
coast ranges of California and the Northwest. Outside of
Alaska, only thirty-five million American acres are set aside
as designated wilderness—1.8 percent of the lower forty-
eight. Additional designations over the next few years may
raise the total to 3 percent.

Few wilderness areas are big enough to absorb a two-
week pack trip, the measure Aldo Leopold proposed as a
minimum standard. Many of them fail even to meet Bob
Marshall's laxer requirement that a wilderness be big
enough that it can't be crossed in one day without mechan-

ical help. In the Mount Jefferson Wilderness I could look
eastward down the Whitewater River to a patchwork of
irrigated pasture and cropland, then amble across Jefferson
Park in half an hour and gaze westward at the hazy blue
curves of the lower Cascades, blotched with a spreading
mange of clearcuts. Mount Jefferson is a designated wilderness partly because our culture sees beauty in snowy crags
and alpine meadows, but mainly because such terrain offers
few exploitable resources to contemporary Thomas Mortons
and is hard to enter with machines. Like other members of
the wilderness system, Mount Jefferson is a small, expendable leaving passed over by the engines of commerce.

Even as such, however, protected lands are not entirely
free of commercial exploitation. Though wilderness is de-
fined by law as land "where the earth and its community of
life are untrammeled by man," national forest wilderness
areas were open to new mining claims for a full twenty years
after the law was passed. Claims have been filed in probably
every wilderness and wilderness study area in the West, and
some host active mining operations. As for those whose
business is the mining of trees, in the Northwest they cut
right up to, and occasionally across, wilderness boundaries.
And wilderness areas throughout the interior West are
freely trampled by swarms of cows that foul springs, muck
up meadows, and generously splat the land with their met-
abolic produce on their way to becoming a minuscule portion of our annual beef.

But it isn't miners or bovines who pose the greatest danger to wilderness. It's the throngs of us two-legged solitude-seekers who flood the high backcountry every summer, plodding happily beneath our ponderous loads. Bradford and Mather would rejoice to see how thoroughly we are humanizing the alien, devil-infested land—how we brighten the weather-beaten hues of nature with Gore-Tex and ripstop nylon in all shades and brightnesses, how we enliven the dismal mountain silences with the clatter of aluminum cookware and our ebullient talk. We do indeed need the tonic of wildness, and more and more of us seem bound and determined to have it at the same time.

My trip to Mount Jefferson lasted into a weekend, and as Saturday morning turned to afternoon, the meadow of Jefferson Park fairly flowed with fresh hikers drawn by the delightful October sun. They strode, ambled, and talked continually past my camp—where I sat solemnly reading in Thoreau's *Journal* on the virtues of solitude—until I tired of exchanging pleasantries and loaded my pack. It took two hours to find a grassy spot sheltered by rocks where I could avoid the sight, if not the sounds, of my fellow nature lovers, and grouse in peace about the violation of *my* wilderness.

Place of wild beasts, indeed. Any bear or mountain lion in its right mind stayed miles away from Jefferson Park that weekend. It was a human village, and except for those who came purposely to place themselves in danger by climbing the mountain, no one there faced any jeopardy more dire than the possibility of contracting giardiasis from the water—which was likely contaminated, in part, by human beings—or twisting an ankle on one of the trails that crisscross the meadow. Should an injury have occurred, helicopters were not far away, ready to evacuate the unfortunate—one of them blatted overhead, in fact, during the hush of alpenglow one evening. The condition of *bewilderment* that Bradford and his Pilgrims experienced at Cape Cod, uncertainty laced with mortal fear and awe, was not remotely available to anyone in Jefferson Park that weekend. That place at that time was a wilderness only on the maps we all carried.

And the diminishment of the wilderness experience, of course, corresponds to a diminishment of the land itself. Much is said and written these days about traceless camping, walking softly upon the earth and leaving only footprints, but popular backcountry destinations are looking worse and worse. Toilet paper blooms from beneath stones, bottles and cans shine in the beds of streams, snags are torn to pieces and living trees stripped for firewood, which is burned in multiple fire rings dotting the meadows and groves. And footsteps alone, in sufficient numbers, do plenty of damage. They destroy delicate ground vegetation, leave barren and compacted soil in camp areas and around lakes, and wear trails into ditches which are then abandoned for new trails alongside, resulting in multilane wilderness freeways. Pack horses amplify the people-pressure by enabling large parties to enjoy long stays in the wild, and their hooves are hard on streambanks. Mountain bikers, though legally barred from wilderness, whip around at will in many areas, only too happy to pay a citation—if they are unlucky enough to be caught—as a cheap price for their fun.

Small wilderness areas not far from big cities, such as Mount Jefferson, show the effects of human visitation first and most severely. But as the population grows, as the remaining unprotected wild areas are roaded and logged and mined, as backpackers, turned off by the crowds, travel farther and farther for their adventure and solitude, the larger and more remote wild places will inevitably suffer wear—the Bob Marshall, the Selway-Bitterroot, the River of No Return. Setting aside new wilderness areas may temporarily relieve some of the pressure, but there is a limited supply of roadless acreage suitable for designation, and the economic interests opposed to more wilderness are formidable. What's more, designating a place makes it an immediate target for recreational use. The words "wilderness area" on a map exert a talismanic power, drawing hordes of lovers eager to experience the charms of new land.

The American conservation movement, better known for its intelligence and eloquence than for its successes, has in this one way succeeded all too well. John Muir saw at the turn of the century that the fate of wild places depended on people knowing they were there, and thus the Sierra Club was born, organizing outings so that city dwellers might experience the backcountry and fight to save it. The belief that access to wild nature is essential to our human lives has always been a central assumption of the movement that won the Wilderness Act and has sought to expand the wilderness system since. That belief has intensified as our society grows increasingly urban and industrial. It is a love charged by displacement, a longing to save what we have left behind. And it grinds us, increasingly, in the jaws of a contradiction.

The Forest Service estimates, at usage rates projected from the present, that by the year 2040 the Mount Jefferson Wilderness may be receiving the impact of 225,000 visitor days per year. A visitor day is one person spending twelve hours in the wilderness. The current impact is in the neighborhood of 83,000 visitor days, already exceeding the 70,000 capacity that one Forest Service spokesman figures for the place—numbers grim enough in themselves, considering that Mount Jefferson is a small area of only 100,000 acres and that most of its use is focused in one spot, the scenic Jefferson Park. After a public advisory process, the Forest Service has decided to institute a permit system to limit use of Mount Jefferson and two adjacent wilderness areas, Mount Washington and Three Sisters. Permit systems are already in place in several other wilderness areas across the country.

To impose such controls—to impose *any* control on wilderness access—seems to strike at the heart of the freedom we have always associated with unsettled places. You don't check with the government when you're itchy to light out for the territories, you just go. But we don't have the territories anymore, we have this ragbag of small wild leavings, and the law that sets them aside says they are to be untrammeled by human beings. Habitations and motor vehicles disrupt the wild communities, and so they are barred. If backpackers and pack trains and climbers and day-hikers are disruptive as well, it makes sense under the law, and out of respect for the land, to limit their entry to a level the land can bear.

It makes sense, that is, if the main purpose of wilderness designation is to preserve land in an unimpaired state. If, on the other hand, its main purpose is to provide backcountry recreation to the American people, limiting our access makes little sense. The Wilderness Act clearly cites *both* purposes, providing that wilderness areas "shall be administered for the use and enjoyment of the American people," but "in such manner as will leave them unimpaired for future use and enjoyment as wilderness." So far, the Forest Service and other wilderness managers have been able, by and large, to accommodate both aims. But the evidence from Mount Jefferson, and from other heavily visited members of the system, is that wilderness enjoyment and wilderness preservation are going to conflict increasingly as goals for the land.

In the management of public lands other than wilderness, human use and enjoyment has almost invariably received priority over the integrity of the land—mainly Thomas Morton's kind of enjoyment, the forcible extraction of the land's natural endowments. In our national forests, for the last forty years at least, logging has come first, other uses and values far behind. That emphasis has now begun to change, but it changes slowly. In the public domain of the Bureau of Land Management, mining, grazing, logging, and oil and gas drilling are considered the highest uses of the natural world. Even the refuge system of the U.S. Fish and Wildlife Service is by no means exclusively protective of the wild communities—all the aforementioned enjoyments occur there too, and it is an open question, especially in the fall, whether waterfowl refuges are managed for ducks or for hunters of ducks.

In the National Park System, oriented from its beginnings toward preservation rather than exploitation, extractive activities are banned or severely limited. But the Park Service has in its charter the same conflicted charge contained in the Wilderness Act—provide for the people's enjoyment but leave the land unimpaired—and in the most popular parks, where the conflict began to manifest itself in the sixties, the Park Service has tilted markedly toward people. There can be no question that in places such as Yosemite Valley, which every summer becomes a smoggy city overrun by millions of visitors and their cars, both the experience of nature and the land itself are being impaired.

The Park Service responded in the seventies by developing a Yosemite master plan that would phase out automobile access and many existing buildings. The plan was never implemented. Apparently the government has decided not to make a decision on Yosemite's future, and the crowds grow every year.

Those who manage the National Wilderness Preservation System are tilting the other way, toward preserving the land in its wholeness, and it is exactly right that they should. In creating the wilderness system, our society had a new idea in mind. We realized that in peopling and subduing the land we were in danger of losing it, and so we drew boundaries around a few primeval patches of a carved-up continent, a few remnant places where nature might go on working as it used to work before the carvers came along. That was a visionary act of collective self-restraint. If we truly believe in keeping those lands untrammeled by man, we should be prepared to extend our self-restraint just as far as necessary. A permit system in heavily-used areas is a small price to pay for the health of the last wild lands we will ever have.

It may be that we will need to accept severer limits. Permit systems may simply perpetuate a condition of marginal overuse and land degradation. In badly damaged areas, it may become necessary to bar human beings altogether—for ten or twenty or fifty years, for as long as it takes the injured land to restore itself. Wallace Stegner, in his "Wilderness Letter," argues that the *idea* of wilderness, simply knowing it is there in its health and wholeness, is ultimately worth more than any use, recreational or extractive, we might make of it. His view offers an appropriate guide for protecting wilderness from its lovers. I would miss Jefferson Park if I couldn't go there again, but I know very well that what that place needs is relief from human beings. And though I would miss it, I would be pleased to think of the fire rings and the crisscross of trails healing over with grass and huckleberries, the mountain lions returning, the waters running and winds blowing in the quiet of the land.

I hope we are capable of respecting our wild places enough to leave them alone. But even if no human beings set foot in a wilderness area again, those lands would still suffer harm. The threat we pose to them is both more complicated and more dangerous than the pounding of our boots. In the time when Aldo Leopold and Bob Marshall were pioneering the concept of wilderness, even in 1964 when the Wilderness Act was passed, it was possible to believe that drawing a boundary around a piece of land was sufficient to protect it. We know differently now. We know that no boundary can block the ozone and other internal combustion pollutants borne downwind from Seattle and Portland and Los Angeles, poisons that disrupt photosynthesis and make trees more vulnerable to other stresses in their environment. And no line on a map can ward off the acid fog and precipitation now occurring in parts of the

Cascades and the Sierra Nevada at levels shown to have damaged forests under experimental conditions, and at lower but probably increasing levels in places as remote as the Wind River Range of Wyoming.

The tonic of wilderness has been tainted. The air breathed by trees and humans is not the air that Thoreau breathed, and it is not getting any purer. Carbon dioxide in the atmosphere has increased by 25 percent in the last hundred years, and at current rates of accumulation will double in the next century. Other greenhouse gases are also building up. The exact effect they will have on the planet is impossible to predict, but that they will have an effect is certain. An average temperature increase of three to eight degrees Fahrenheit is possible. In the American West, the mountain snowline could rise by as much as three thousand feet, and a region already characterized by aridity could face a 15-to-20-percent reduction in the moisture that sustains it. Many species of plants and animals could disappear. Forested land would shrink along with the snowpack, and as the region rapidly dried, forest fires bigger than those of the eighties could become commonplace.

The impact of global warming could be lesser, or harsher, or different in ways no one can foresee. But it should be clear by now, in any case, that the industrial-technological road we have taken is a dangerous one, and it forces us to reconsider what we mean by wilderness. To set aside areas of unspoiled land was, and remains, the necessary first step. The second, just as necessary, is to recognize that the fate of wilderness is deeply entangled with our own. Trees, animals, humans, we are all endangered. The act of self-restraint required of us involves more than simply halting our cars or even our footsteps at the wilderness boundary —we need to restrain the reckless way of life that first made that boundary necessary and now threatens to make it meaningless. If we fail to do that, what William Bradford and Cotton Mather feared may come to pass: nature may turn on us and destroy us. But it won't be the devil in the guise of a bird or thunderstorm who brings our ruin, it will be the two-legged stranger we scarcely understand, the one wild beast we seem unable to bring under control.

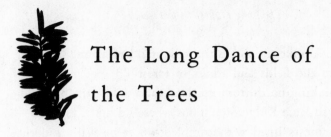

The Long Dance of
the Trees

MANY YEARS AGO on Washington's
Olympic Peninsula, eager to penetrate the depths of a western wilderness, I veered off the Hoh River trail into rainforest. The spruces and hemlocks closed around me. Ferns sopped my pants. Thick vines sloped across my way, clotheslining my brand-new backpack stuffed with a week's worth of food. In the solemn forest light I stepped uncertainly, guiltily, each footfall crushing delicate layerings of bright green moss, moss that covered everything above ground as well—the enormous trunks and broken snags, the vines, the fallen rotting logs over which I awkwardly clambered. I didn't know where I was going in that slippery strew of life, but I soon realized I wasn't going far. Dropping my pack, I climbed on top of a log some five feet through.

In the sudden absence of my own noise, the huge quiet pressed in. It was raining lightly, soundlessly, no breath of wind, no bird, no animal sound. Something a little unsettling, something tinged with fear, replaced my exploring ardor. Unlike the woods the wide trail had led me through, unlike the fields and fronts of forest I'd sped past while hitchhiking north from Portland, and unlike the bramble-patched Blue Ridge Mountains where I'd hiked as a kid— leafy forests lined with tumbledown stone walls and the ghosts of old mail roads—this place was touched by nothing human. This wet green riot didn't know who I was, and didn't especially welcome me. But as much as it disturbed me it also thrilled me, struck a happy thoughtless glow in my gut. I leaned over and stuck my nose into the mossy log, into its sodden crumbling wood-dirt, into the thick black smell of it. To either side of me, all down the log's fifty-foot length, seedlings and saplings were growing out of it in a straight line. I sat with them a long time, shoulder to shoulder, full of a strange and familiar contentment.

I was in my first old-growth forest—a forest, I learned later, that exceeds even the tropical jungles in its acre-for-acre production of living material. I didn't have a name for it then, and neither did I connect the forest around me with the mountains farther south in the state that I was helping to shear. That summer, and most of the next, I was a choker-setter for the Weyerhaeuser Timber Company, playing a game of colossal pickup sticks called high-lead logging. After the cutters had dropped all the trees on a slope and bucked them into lengths, the rest of us set to work hitching the logs to a cable rigging to be reeled up the hill by a diesel yarder equipped with a hundred-foot steel tower. The logs were mostly two or three feet in diameter, but occasionally we came upon what had.been an ancient stand of red cedar, Douglas fir, or western hemlock, the butt-cuts sometimes ten or twelve feet through. A choker cable would snap like string on one of those giants, so we cradled that kind in a two-choker wrap. Then we cleared out of the way, watching it lurch from its bed and start stubbornly up the hill as the yarder roared, the log plunging and rolling like a huge hooked fish, scattering smaller logs and uprooting stumps and gouging long raw grooves in the wet earth. We whooped and hollered and cheered the log on, and when the rigging came back we hooked up another, and another, and on through the days until the hillside was nothing but stumps and dirt and thickets of limb-trash.

I was vaguely uneasy with all that destruction, but mainly I was pleased to be working as a logger, to be wearing suspenders and a tin hard hat, learning to chew plug and cuss well and drink great quantities of beer. Occasionally, I felt a twinge. One day we ate lunch by a fern-bordered runnel that wound its way down the desolate slope and splashed over rocks where we sat. It looked all wrong in the clearcut's noon glare—muddy, misdirected, out of place. I tried to imagine it as it once must have been, how its small splashing might have sounded in the shadowy groves, how the elk might have stopped to drink and passed on. The stream had once been part of the forest's mysterious life. Now it was a trivial oddity, discolored and tawdry, scarcely audible above the diesel's idle.

Weyerhaeuser laid waste to those Washington hills, and in the process wasted nothing. We spent many cold minutes grubbing choker-holes under mud-buried logs. If a rotted log looked close to half good, we choked it. If a chunk was thicker than six inches and longer than eight feet, we choked it. The hooktender—boss of the crew—prowled the barren slope behind us for pieces we should have sent up the hill. Waste is against the logger's religion. Wood left on the ground will never become lumber or paper, never become money, and the same applies to standing timber left past its prime. To the wood-products man an old-growth forest, with its many dead and dying trees, is an over-mature forest, a decadent forest, a forest in decline doing no human being any good. As a Reagan administration official is said to have remarked, "Old-growth forests remind me of an old folks home, just waiting to die."

He said that because he sees board footage when he looks at trees. He sees rotation cycles and allowable annual cuts, he sees lumber and houses and an ill-defined picture of progress that he takes to be the future because it has been the past. To be fair, since clearly he is a man of poetical instincts, he probably sees some beauty in ancient trees, and he probably appreciates that woodpeckers and other creatures nest and feed in them. But he doesn't see, or if he sees he doesn't appreciate, the slow exuberant dance the forest does through time. He doesn't see the intricate webwork of fungi that strands through the ground, drawing its food from the roots of trees and helping the roots draw food from the soil. He doesn't see the red-backed vole that eats the fungi's fruiting bodies and disperses their spores, sheltering itself in downed rotting wood. He doesn't see the spotted owl that eats the red-backed vole, hunting through thousands of acres of forest, feeding her owlets high in the limbs, as all around the trees keep growing and each in its turn goes down, melting into ground, sheltering the vole and feeding the fungi and holding the cold rainwater in its fragrant sponge.

That is one movement of one forest's dance. Countless such movements looping together form the dynamic equilibrium that is old-growth forest. It expresses itself differently in different regions, from the coastal groves of California redwoods to the shrinking pine forests of eastern Oregon to pockets of Douglas fir in the northern Rockies to what is left of the North Woods of the Great Lake states to a few hardwood patches in New Hampshire's White Mountains to sixty-five acres of virgin white oaks in Franklin Township, New Jersey, that grow within sight of the World Trade Center. Outside of Alaska, old growth in America is mostly a scatter of small remnants. Ninety percent of the forests that originally flourished have been humanly altered or have vanished. Only in the Pacific

Northwest do extensive tracts of old growth remain, most of them in the Douglas fir belt that runs the Coast Range and the west slope of the Cascades through Washington, Oregon, and northwestern California.

Unlike young and mature forests, old growth in the Northwest is a vigorous diversity of tree species and sizes, including massive Douglas firs that approach three hundred feet in height and thirty feet in circumference at the base. Beneath these giants grow smaller trees, sometimes giants themselves—western hemlock, red cedar, big-leaf maple, and other shade-tolerant species, the trees together forming an uneven canopy that diffuses light into an ample soft radiance. Because shrubs, herbs, and seedlings are usually sparse and patchy, the forest seems spacious, deep to the eye. And everywhere, more various even than their living progeny, are the generations of trees gone by—the standing dead with dry needles still intact, limbless snags, rotting stubs coated with moss, and downed logs and limbs of all sizes and stages of decay.

The Douglas firs begin as seedling pioneers in an area opened by fire or other disturbance, growing quickly for a hundred years, more slowly for another hundred. During that time each tree looks much like the others, a stand of uniform cousins, but after two centuries a combination of genetic inheritance, competition with neighbors, and the scarrings of storm and fire shapes each tree into a distinct individual. The great trunk, pocked with cavities, tilts at an angle. Often the top is broken, and the tree's crown is a bottle-brush of short, unevenly spaced branches, many of them fanlike sprays growing out of the broken stubs of older branches. The bark is deeply furrowed, mossy, and often charred near the ground.

Practically every surface of every tree is colonized by lichens and mosses, over a hundred separate species in all, some of which fix nitrogen from the air and draw minerals from rainwater, storing the nutrients and slowly contributing them to the entire forest through leaching and litter-fall. The upper surfaces of large branches become ecosystems of their own, accumulating a soil of organic debris that supports entire communities of plants and invertebrate animals. In all, over fifteen hundred species of invertebrates can inhabit the canopy of an old-growth stand, as well as such vertebrates as the red tree vole, many generations of which will often remain in a single tree. In winter the canopy keeps the ground clear of heavy snow, and its water content—a quarter of a million gallons per acre—softens the effects of hard weather, providing refuge for deer and elk and other wildlife species.

A Douglas fir can live for a thousand years, and its contribution to the forest far outlives the tree. Dozens of species of birds and mammals use standing snags for nesting, courtship displays, and sources of food. Specific animals require snags at specific stages of decay, and old-growth forest provides the entire range—just as it provides an array of downed logs, from intact wind-thrown trees to barely perceptible linear mounds on the forest floor, the remains of five hundred years of decomposition. Logs are used in even more ways than snags: they are cover, bedding, lookout, pathway, food source, and food storage for hundreds of varieties of birds, amphibians, and mammals. Several animals, including the marten, fisher, and northern spotted owl, probably require old-growth forest for their long-term survival. Old growth is preferred habitat for some forty other species, and hundreds more use it for various purposes at certain times in their lives.

Many plant species as well find optimal conditions in old-growth forest, and some very likely need it to survive. The rotting wood of downed trunks provides a receptive site for the germination and growth of young plants and trees, and one of the most remarkable relationships of the old-growth system takes place there. Mycorrhizal fungi colonize the logs and attach themselves to seedling tree roots in a bond that means life to both. Tapping the roots for their stored sugars, the mycorrhizae enzymatically break down nutrient compounds in the rotting wood that the seedlings are incapable of processing themselves—chemically they crack the nut and present the kernel to their hungry hosts. Long after the nurse log has merged into ground, sometimes leaving a straight colonnade of adult trees, the fungi continue to pass nutrients from soil to roots.

The mushrooms and truffles that appear on logs and in

needle duff, eaten and scattered by small mammals, are the fungi's fruiting bodies—all that shows of the gossamer webwork pursuing its commerce underground. The old-growth economy works mainly out of sight. Rotting logs are the fundament of that economy, powering and stabilizing the entire system through their slow decay. Energy, nutrients, and organic materials that were gradually gathered by living trees are gradually released to the use of other plants and animals. Water is conserved in ground debris, and fallen trunks and limbs restrain the erosive power of streams, creating pool habitats such as spawning gravels for salmon. With the passage of organic matter kept slow, entire food chains have a chance to flourish, and a steady renewal of pure water feeds the streams and rivers and towns of the Pacific Northwest.

Conservation is the genius of the old-growth economy. Nothing is wasted—but unlike the logger who takes everything out, the old-growth system keeps everything in. The death and dying that so depress the government official are part of a continuous cycling pathway of life, dead life going down to the darkness of soil and new life rising to the sun, looping streams of energy that look to us like stillness and sound like the most profound quiet. To the official, the forest is wasted commodity. To John Muir, who wasn't much interested in board footage, it was a self-renewing fountain where his spirit could drink: "The woods are full of dead and dying trees, yet needed for their beauty to complete the beauty of the living. . . . How beautiful is all Death!"

Clearly Muir's is the richer, more imaginative view. But the government official, within the purview of his specialized mind, sees truly. He would break the long dance of the trees because humans require what trees are made of. Because I write these words on the stuff of trees, because I sit on dead trees to write them, because dead trees carry John Muir's thoughts across a hundred years to my eyes, I can't discount the official's view. We use trees. We need to cut them. And we need to decide, while we still have a choice, where the line should be drawn between our needs and the last of the old-growth forest.

Once, except for the disruptions of fire and other natural catastrophes, it was all old growth. And ever since John Smith and his settlers arrived in Virginia to find "faire meadows and goodly tall Trees," we've been steadily engaged in cutting it down. The great white pines, which often soared over two hundred feet, were the tallest and the first to fall. Thomas Morton, an early colonizer of Massachusetts, wrote to England that the New World supported an "infinite store" of the pines. Felled for boards and boat planks and flawless masts for the king's navy, they were quickly gone. The mixed hardwoods that shouldered the pines formed a wild so unbroken, the legend goes, that a squirrel with a sense of purpose could have traveled from the Atlantic to the Mississippi without touching ground. Few settlers facing that vast woods had the foresight of William Penn, who ordered one acre of trees left standing for every five cut. We pursued our future and the endless forest was left in fragments, eaten by axes, intentionally burned when ash was more valuable than lumber. Throughout the nineteenth century, timbering boomed as our busiest trade, finishing off the eastern forest, the North Woods of Minnesota and Wisconsin, the southern pines and hardwoods, and then setting to work in California, where John Muir saw sequoias blasted down with gunpowder, the massive trunks half-shattered into useless splinters. And today, across the Northwest and the Rockies, less wastefully but every bit as wasting, the clearcutting continues, reducing what is left of the primeval American forest to unstable soils, thickets of brush, and orderly ranks of planted trees.

Logged areas in the Northwest were replanted haphazardly, or not at all, for the first half of this century; only since the fifties, as sustained yield has developed as a goal if not a fact, has reforestation intensified. Having cut the old growth on their own lands, and with second-growth crops still decades from maturity, timber corporations have pressed for higher and higher annual cuts on the national forests and other public lands—the lands that contain almost all that remains of old-growth forest in the lower forty-eight states.

Until very recently, the corporations have gotten what

they've wanted. Clearcuts are visible from practically any highway in Douglas fir country, but the highway view is misleadingly benign. Only those who fly over the mountains or climb the high peaks can see how thoroughly the barren patchwork and squiggling white roads have penetrated the green hills, and only those who drive those logging roads can see how destructive a clearcut can be. Slopes nearly as steep as cliffs have been sheared, and with nothing to secure it the soil is going, slumping and silting the streams, leaving open wounds in the watersheds. Such slopes were logged with no thought for what the land could bear. They were logged to make cash of their trees, a one-time bonanza centuries in the making. They weren't harvested, they were mined. And as tree-mining slashes its way through the backcountry, much of the remaining forest is left in pieces, susceptible to windthrow and diminished as habitat.

The damage that clearcuts do isn't necessarily conspicuous. A gentle hillside cropped of its growth and planted in bright young Douglas firs is not an unpleasant sight. Deer and elk are fond of the browse such openings temporarily provide, and the trees grow quickly. But the forest they become bears little resemblance, visually or ecologically, to the forest that was stripped—it is a single-species forest of same-age trees, a forest robbed of the organic material so crucial to the old-growth system, a forest biologically barren compared to the teeming diversity it has replaced. The ecological complexities of old growth, including its unique qualities as habitat and watershed, take at least 175 years to begin to develop. The planted clearcuts will be harvested in less than a century, as soon as the trees finish their surge of adolescent growth. Trees, as the industry platitude goes, are a renewable resource. But old-growth forest is not.

Today, in the national forests of Douglas fir country, less than 15 percent of the original old-growth forest is left. Much of that remainder has been riddled with clearcuts, leaving the forest in fragments. Very few major stands of old growth remain, and the controversy that first arose in the eighties—regionally, then nationally—centers on those last ecologically viable stands: whether to log them heavily, as the industry wants and as national forest plans allow, or to protect much of them in old-growth preserves, as conservationists want. For now, conservationists are prevailing. Logging has been sharply reduced in the Douglas fir forests of the public lands. But the reduction didn't result from a sudden recognition of the aesthetic beauty and ecological value of old-growth forest. It occurred because federal forest managers were directed by court orders to secure the old-growth habitat of a particular threatened species, the northern spotted owl.

For the forest, such protection is tenuous at best. The owl could be taken off the threatened list if studies find its population is higher than was thought, or if it is found to be less dependent on old growth than was thought. The Endangered Species Act or other existing federal legislation might be amended or repealed in order to free the enjoined lands for timber cutting. And the logging slowdown west of the Cascade crest has only intensified logging east of the crest, in the old-growth forests of ponderosa pine where no spotted owl stands in the way. The remnant ancient forests of the Pacific Northwest won't be secure until they are valued not as habitat for a particular rare bird, but as communities of life that many species, including our own, have an interest in sustaining. Neither owl nor forest is likely to survive unless the human economy of the Northwest embraces a new way of valuing the natural economy that makes it possible.

Historically, in the East and the lake states and the South, timber has been a nomadic and volatile industry, moving into a region and stripping the trees and moving on. In the Northwest the boom is over. After a century of logging, most by far of the original forest inheritance is gone. The industry is already shifting its focus back to the Southeast, where operating costs are less and the climate and terrain are more conducive to the growing of trees as crops. The Northwest will continue to produce timber, but the spotted-owl injunctions have accelerated a necessary change in how it produces and how much—the change from an economy based on rampant consumption of one of the greatest forests on Earth to a more diversified economy in which timber plays only such a role as the land can sustain. The fate of old growth depends on how soon and how thoroughly that change is accepted. Even if Congress does create a system of old-growth preserves, those islands of intact forest will mean little—and might not survive—if the forest lands around them suffer continued devastation from the practices of the past.

In a sustainable timbering economy, a tree will be cut only when another tree reaches maturity, and only in a way that doesn't damage the capacity of the land to grow trees. Further—and this is already beginning to happen—forest managers will look to old growth as the model for a healthy forest, moving away from monocultures, even-age management, and the Germanic preoccupation with order and cleanliness that has dominated American forestry from the beginning. The work of restoring the Douglas fir ecosystem will create new jobs, replacing some of those lost as the old regime passes. And more jobs will be created when the Northwest stops allowing itself to be used as a colonial economy, supplying raw logs and minimally processed building materials to the rest of the country and the world, and becomes instead a manufacturing center for furniture, fine millwork, and other finished products. As the old-growth system slows the passage of nutrients and water, thus enabling complete food chains to flourish, so the Northwest needs to slow the passage of its timber to feed the economic life of its communities.

It is often argued that Northwest timber production can't be reduced permanently without diminishing economic prosperity in the region and perhaps the nation, that we must keep clearcutting the national forests to support the economic growth we're accustomed to. It may well be true. But the old-growth trees that are left would feed the saws only for another twenty or thirty years, time that would be better spent facing a fact we have long ignored: if the land can't afford the economic growth we're accustomed to, we can't afford it either. Stripped mountainsides don't signify prosperity, they signify poverty. They tell us, or they should tell us, that the kind of growth we hold practically sacred is in fact a self-centered adolescence we'd do well to put behind us. In the Douglas fir forest, rapid growth gives way after a hundred years to slower growth and then an equilibrium of growth and death, gain and loss, the forest's wealth conserved and carefully recycled. Each member of the community is supported by what the land in its health allows, a diverse and vigorous commonwealth sustaining itself through time. It is a way of living more stable and more sensible than our own, a way of living that we could be instructed by, if we could stop ourselves from turning it into two-by-fours and more tract homes.

John Muir wrote: "We all travel the Milky Way together, trees and men." Defying our anthropocentric tradition, he places trees and humans on an equal footing and joins the two in a single "We," a single band of travelers. Muir understood, not merely with his intellect but with the full vitality of his imagination, that trees and humans are bound together in one planetary matrix of life, realizing itself through billions of years. We are here together, sharing both origin and future.

Something happened to me, something that has helped me grow, in the stillness of that Olympic rainforest. And something happened to me at ten thousand feet in the White Mountains of California, in the airy groves of bristlecone pines. Some of them as old as 4,600 years, oldest of all trees, they grow in a few colonies surrounded by sky, their roots clenched deep in crevices of stone. Windscoured, split open by lightning, showing more bare grain than bark, they still put out sprays of their stubby green needles. Each tree is a complete record of all it has been, dwarfed and twisted but fully formed, fully present in the world. In their individual aging you can see their age as a kind, the long conifer trail they have traveled to their few mountaintops from a time well before the birth of the broadleafs, from the time when plants were first colonizing land. On rocky peaks across the Great Basin the bristlecones go on, answering snow, sun, and centuries with the measured speech of their bright brown cones.

Aldo Leopold, walking among his Wisconsin pines in winter, received from their snowy ranks "a curious transfusion of courage." The bristlecone forest is courage-giving too, adapted as it is to a hard location and developed to distinction, to a complex and perfect rightfulness. There, as in the Olympic rainforest, as in the soaring groves of Douglas fir and open stands of orange-barked pines, I feel the forest keenly as *place*. All old-growth forests, in their different ways, are distinctly placed, and are made of distinct places. A stand of big, tilting, broken-limbed Douglas firs is thick with place; a "Hi-Yield" forest of uniform young trees is not. The muddy runnel that twinged my conscience twenty years ago wasn't a place then, but it had been.

Near a camp I used to visit in south-central Oregon, by Cougar Peak, a stream runs down a shallow valley into Cottonwood Lake. Climbing alongside it, you pass from a grassy bowl scattered with aspens into a woods of big white fir and ponderosa pine. It's not a striking forest, no one view of more interest than another, until you come to a great pine fallen across the stream. A shallow pool has formed behind it. Streamwater has saturated the trunk and slowly found seepways through it, spilling out the downstream side and carving the grain over time into a delicate mosaic of points and whorls. Mosses, ferns, and small yellow flowers grow out of the log, fed by the steady trickling, bright and shaded in the filtered light. You stop there, you listen. You touch the spongy mosses, you peer into the log's crevices, you sit a while if the mosquitoes aren't too bad. That over-mature tree, with all its wasted board footage, has in dying given birth to a place.

In time the log will rot through and the little cosmos of the pool will revert to flowing stream. Heard or unheard by humans, other trees will fall. More pools will form, like the earlier one and different. The firs and pines will grow and go down, grow and go down: Seedlings will rise where light allows them, curled beneath snow, springing up with the melt, raising themselves through the turning of seasons alongside the dead trunks merging into ground. Birds and insects will nest in the snags, deer will carefully step their way, the cougar will stalk and make its kills, the wind will play through the boughs of pines as clouds cross the sky, and all will change in the hands of time toward whatever it will become. In forest, Earth speaks a peculiar profusion, a birthing ground of possibility.

And we ourselves are acquainted with possibility. There was another forest, a forest I haven't seen for a very long time, a forest of tall broadleaf trees on a great flatland, interwoven into one spreading crown broken by patches of grassy plain. There was stillness upon it—but as in all forest, stillness contained the movements of life. Birds called and flicked through the boughs, insects were at home on trunks and limbs, and something else moved, something that had lived in trees for millions of years. In that distance of time, slowly, its paws had blossomed with fingers and thumb. Slowly its eyes had aligned in the front of its head, so that each graspable branch stood clear as it swung and leaped the high pathways. And slowly the monochrome world had flared with color, deepened with the clarity and beauty of things—leaves, fruit, and the tawny grasses beneath the trees where one day this animal would wander, the long ground it would travel on its way to the winning of the world.

We are the children of those African trees. Whatever we are, they helped make us. We sense when we enter a still depth of forest what Emerson sensed in the Concord horizon, something as beautiful as our own nature, something, indeed, of our nature itself. We travel the Milky Way together, trees and humans, and before we destroy what is left of the world's old forests, we might pause to ask whose limbs we are lopping, whose skin we are stripping, whose bodies we are severing from their roots in the ground. We might pause to ask, as our past perishes in the screech of saws, if we aren't at the same time clearcutting our future from the face of the earth.

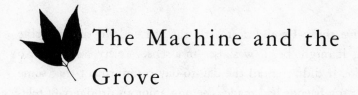

The Machine and the Grove

I HAVE COMMITTED civil disobedience twice. In 1968, because I believed in neither the draft nor the war in Vietnam, I mailed my draft card to the director of the Selective Service System and refused induction into the U.S. Army. I was expecting to stand trial and to go to jail—white middle-class resisters were getting eighteen to twenty-four months—but, for reasons I haven't tried to discover, I was never indicted. Ten years later I was part of a large group of demonstrators who climbed a fence onto the grounds of the Trojan nuclear power plant in Oregon in an effort to call attention to the dangers of that and all nuclear plants. I spent three days in jail, and was convicted of second-degree criminal trespass and sentenced to three days of community service.

In both cases I believed intensely in a cause, and in both cases I had divided feelings about the means that I and others had chosen. Refusing induction was the purest and most dramatic act I could think of to protest the war. Maybe it was even noble, I felt. But was it the most effective thing I could do to end the war and the draft? Noble as it might be, it was also, in a sense, a very easy thing to do. It didn't entail the day-to-day commitment that some of my friends had made, the unglamorous drudgery of telephones and mailing lists and tacking up posters. I would make my clean gesture, stand trial with dignity, and serve my time in prison—where, in my twenty-year-old mind, I hoped I would be allowed to practice classical guitar all day for two years.

My second thoughts about the nuclear protest came mostly after the fact. I saw some news footage of our occupation, and of occupations at other nuclear plants around the country that summer, and I wondered just how many American hearts and minds would be won to our cause by the spectacle of a swarm of young people—many, like me, with beards and other signs of the sixties—climbing a fence, sitting on the innocuous green lawn of a spick-and-span power plant, and singing songs as the cops dragged us away and put the cuffs on us. Somehow we didn't have the dignity—and I wondered if we had one-tenth the commitment—of the civil rights demonstrators whose sit-ins we were mimicking. We were concerned about the issue, but how much did we really know? And were some of us, just possibly, more excited about breaking the law and drawing attention to ourselves than about closing a nuclear power plant?

In retrospect, it's hard to say what effect those occupations had. No additional nuclear plants have been built in this country since 1978, but that could be due entirely to the accidents at Three Mile Island and Chernobyl. Maybe the direct action protests during the seventies and eighties helped in some way to turn the social climate against expansion of nuclear power. Maybe they didn't.

In the environmental movement as a whole, civil disobedience—I mean the term to include all forms of law breaking and unconventional direct action in pursuit of a cause—has become increasingly common in the last twenty years, and my feelings have remained divided. Certain cases I feel clear about. I've never had the least doubt about the campaigns of Greenpeace, for instance. Its nonviolent interventions against whaling, the harp seal hunt, and polluting chemical plants have been brave and well conceived, and clearly they have both raised public consciousness and directly deterred some of the abuses they have aimed at. But whales are the least controversial of environmental causes, and many Greenpeace actions have occurred at sea against foreign exploiters. In the eighties another wave of environmental radicalism came to the American land itself, directed at many of the same issues that preoccupy traditional conservation groups, but with very different tactics—clandestine missions to spike trees, sabotage machinery, cut down electrical towers, and generally wreak what its practitioners call "miscellaneous deviltry."

This kind of direct action is known as "ecotage," or, less formally, as "monkeywrenching"—a term derived from Edward Abbey's novel *The Monkey Wrench Gang,* which serves the new movement as model and inspiration. Some monkeywrenching is directed against mining and drilling operations in the Southwest and Great Basin; some of it aims to protect the last stands of old-growth forest in California and the Northwest; some of it attacks power plants, billboards, new roads, new construction, any and all symptoms of the exploitive growth economy at work. But ecotage is only one tool of the new radicalism. Many in the movement express themselves, like Greenpeace and the civil rights demonstrators, through nonviolent action—sitting in roadways, chaining themselves to heavy machinery, camping in the branches of threatened trees and remaining for days or weeks. Some of these nonviolent protestors have placed themselves in considerable danger. Many have been arrested and prosecuted, some of them many times.

The slippery center of the new environmental radicalism has been Earth First!, a loosely structured alliance of local groups scattered across the country, though concentrated in the West.* Because Earth First! is anarchical and constantly changing, it resists generalization. Some individuals and local groups do monkeywrenching, some practice passive resistance only. Some abhor politics; some are politically astute and involved. Philosophically, the move-

* In 1990 many original members left Earth First! as the group shifted toward leftist political concerns. What I say in this essay refers to the beliefs and practices of Earth First! as it was constituted in the eighties and as those beliefs and practices continue today under various names.

ment associates itself with the principles of biocentrism, a point of view that sees nature as existing not for humans but for its own sake—humankind as only one element, distinguished mainly by its propensity for ecological disruption, in a planetary matrix of life that has been evolving for three and a half billion years. Mainstream environmentalism, viewed as too anthropocentric and too willing to compromise with the exploiters destroying the land, is held in contempt by many in Earth First! "No Compromise in the Defense of Mother Earth!" is the credo of the movement.

If Earth First! regards traditional conservation groups as complacent, ineffective, and part of the problem, many members of those groups see the new radicals as immature, unrealistic, and either irrelevant or dangerously damaging to the cause, depending on how much trouble they stir up. The constituency of the Sierra Club, the Audubon Society, the Wilderness Society, and other mainstream organizations tend to be upper middle class and higher, comfortable and frequently affluent, somewhat liberal but not to any extreme. They are moderates and gradualists, people who believe in righting environmental wrongs and protecting what it is possible to protect by supporting work through conventional channels: lobbying, litigation, public education. They understand compromise as part of the process. "Not Blind Opposition to Progress, but Opposition to Blind Progress," reads the Sierra Club motto. Many of these environmentalists share my own divided feelings about Earth First!'s monkeywrenching, and about civil disobedience in general. Some think that any lawbreaking is simply wrong.

In short, the radicals and traditionalists of American environmentalism form an uncomfortable alliance at best, and one of the chief causes of discomfort is the issue of civil disobedience. Does it belong in the environmental movement? And if it does, in what situations and in what forms? Among mainstream environmentalists there seems to be some reluctance even to discuss these questions, and this is unfortunate. No harm and a great deal of good might come from airing opinions. I respect and feel allegiance to both the radicals and the traditionalists. Both camps are made up of dedicated men and women doing important work. There is plenty to disagree about. But there is also plenty, it seems to me, to learn from each other.

What might the mainstream learn from the radicals? To begin with, those who are uncomfortable with any form of civil disobedience need to recognize that some believers in any cause will act outside the law, not necessarily because they believe such action will be the most effective, but because conscience compels it in response to a dire and intractable evil. Civil disobedience takes many forms, and some of them may be misguided or counterproductive. But to argue that there is no place in the environmental movement for any illegal act of conscience is to confess that it is less important, and morally less justified, than the civil rights movement or the movement against the Vietnam War.

Environmentalism is every bit as important and justified. It is worth breaking the law to resist violence against the lives and rights of human beings. And it is worth breaking the law to resist violence against the lives and living orders of our planet—because our own lives depend on the health and integrity of those orders, if a selfish reason is necessary, but primarily because nonhuman lives have the right to exist and prosper as well as our own. When John Muir wrote, "We all travel the Milky Way together," he meant trees and all forms of life, not just people. If Muir were alive today, if he were here to witness his beloved forests being stripped from their mountainsides at a rate he couldn't have imagined in his time, he wouldn't restrict himself to testifying at hearings and writing impassioned articles. He would be in the woods with the Earth Firsters.

And what of that other progenitor of the conservation movement, the one who went to jail—if only for one night —rather than support through his taxes a government that condoned human slavery? Would he not have gone to jail to stop the construction of condominiums at Walden Pond? "I think that we should be men first, and subjects afterward," he wrote in *Civil Disobedience*. "It is not desirable to cultivate a respect for the law, so much as for the right." There are times, Thoreau knew well, when one's respect for the right must express itself in extraordinary ways, when normal means of pursuing change are not sufficient: "As for adopting the ways which the State has provided for remedying the evil, I know not of such ways. They take too much time, and a man's life will be gone."

And something else will be gone, the radical environmentalists are telling us. As hearings are held and articles written, as Congress is lobbied and slowly disgorges its halfway measures, as suits are filed and wrangled laboriously in court, the land itself is going. The mainstream skirmishes with the engines of exploitation and wins some battles, defeating a dam here, preserving a small wilderness there, but in no sense is it winning the war. An economy that values wild places only for what they can be made to produce is grinding relentlessly across the public and private lands of America. Grasslands are grazed to dust, deserts staked and gouged open for gold, rivers gripped by multiple dams, forests reduced to fields of stumps. Those who place themselves in front of the machines or attack the machines directly are moved by desperation, by a fierce love for the land that is dying—Muir's love, Thoreau's love, Edward Abbey's love. They express themselves, with or without hope, in the clearest and most forceful ways they can. Civil disobedience is as American as greed, and the environmental movement is one of its rightful homes.

In this regard, I believe, the emergence of environmental radicalism is the best thing that could have happened to the conservation establishment. It warns us that we have compromised the integrity of nature for too long, that the stakes are higher and the hour later than we have allowed ourselves to believe. We have been fighting well and we are losing. Clearly we do not lack experience, intelligence, or dedication. What we need may be the crucial fire of passion, and a willingness to say *no more*. As Gary Snyder writes in a poem:

> *A bulldozer grinding and slobbering*
> *Sideslipping and belching on top of*
> *The skinned-up bodies of still-live bushes*
> *In the pay of a man*
> *From town.*
>
> *Behind is a forest that goes to the Arctic*
> *And a desert that still belongs to the Piute*
> *And here we must draw*
> *Our line.*

To believe in the rightfulness and necessity of civil disobedience, however, is not to believe in the rightfulness and necessity of any illegal act. One who protests the actions of others as a matter of conscience must subject his own actions as well to the rigors of conscience. As Bob Dylan wrote in an early song, "To live outside the law you must be honest." If the normal standards of law and custom are rejected, honesty requires the protester to accept the restraint of self-imposed standards. Anyone can claim the compulsion of conscience. But only those who translate conscience into coherent and principled action make convincing opponents of the evils they hope to change.

The civil rights campaigns of Martin Luther King, Jr., were successful for one reason above all others: without deviation, he and his followers subjected themselves to the standard of nonviolence. They understood that protesters who take violent action against others, no matter what wrong they have suffered or what highminded purpose they hold, destroy their end by their means. Those who sustain the discipline of nonviolent restraint, on the other hand, even in the face of injury and death, are unassailable—they have already won what they are seeking. Dr. King, like Gandhi in India, was able to achieve what he did because he and his followers placed only their own bodies and lives in danger, never the bodies and lives of those they disagreed with.

The power of the principle of nonviolence has not been lost on the radical environmental movement. Those of Earth First! and other groups who sit in front of bulldozers or camp in the branches of trees are placing themselves, like the eco-warriors of Greenpeace, directly in King's tradition. Those who practice monkeywrenching, on the other hand, have chosen to govern themselves by a different standard, a dual standard: no violence against human beings, but all possible violence against the machines of human exploitation.

In the case of one particular form of monkeywrenching, it seems to me that this dual standard is in serious conflict with itself. The practice of tree-spiking is aimed at damaging sawmill machinery, not sawmill workers, but spikers have always known that what they do is potentially harmful to human beings, and in 1987 the potential became actual. In a California mill, a band saw broke on a foot-long spike in a redwood log, breaking the jaw and mutilating the face of a millhand. Earth First! did not plant that spike, but no other group or individual has so publicly and enthusiastically promoted the tactic of tree-spiking. In 1985 the group published an ecotage manual called *Ecodefense: A Field Guide to Monkeywrenching.* Now in its second edition, with well over ten thousand copies in print, the book devotes twenty-eight pages to the techniques of well-concealed tree-spiking, including a refined method that employs pins of stone or ceramic "to defeat the metal detector and wreak havoc inside the sawmill." The book also urges that care be taken "to minimize any possible threat to other people," but the authors of *Ecodefense* can't have it both ways. There are other issues pertaining to the California mill incident— in particular, the poor condition of the saw—but placing steel spikes in the path of saw blades is an inherently dangerous, implicitly violent act. If the authors of *Ecodefense* are serious about their commitment to nonviolence, I hope they will reassess their commitment to tree-spiking, as many in the radical environmental movement have already done.

In other forms of monkeywrenching, machines and structures are damaged or destroyed with no danger to any human being except the saboteurs themselves. The most convincing justification for this practice is one that Martin Luther King would have understood, though he wouldn't have approved of it. When King was criticized, as he was many times, for the violent incidents that some of his peaceful demonstrations touched off, he responded that Jim Crow itself was violence and that his campaigns merely brought the violence out of hiding, exposing Southern society for what it was. Earth First! spokespeople have taken a similar stance, arguing that the real environmental violence in America is being perpetrated by the timber and mining corporations, the dam builders, and the power utilities. The purpose of Earth First!'s commando raids is to make that massive and often irreparable violence visible to the American people.

They are right, of course, that the injuries being done to the American land *are* the primary injuries in question, and their argument cuts to the center of my own divided feelings about civil disobedience. Here is a grove of old-growth trees, and here is a bulldozer, ready to cut a road that will open the grove to logging. The grove is worth infinitely more than the bulldozer. Another machine can be made, but no human being can manufacture a single leaf, let alone an entire tree, let alone the nuanced ecological complexity of the grove. The grove is nature's generativity.

The Machine and the Grove

The bulldozer, as employed here, is an instrument of human destructiveness. I understand the men and women who come in the night to pour grinding compound into the bulldozer's crankcase, who douse the machine with gas and set it on fire. I believe I'm capable of doing it myself, and the time may come when I will. It isn't the worst thing I could do—to do nothing would be far worse. But for two reasons, I don't believe it's the best thing I could do.

First, there are more bulldozers. America has a genius for making big machines, and no shortage of people to run them. The one I incapacitate can be replaced in days, and so can the next one, and the next. In the American economy, the bulldozer is only a small tool, and though it's nice to think that breaking the tool might break the economy, it isn't true. Wrecking the bulldozer might save the grove for a short while, but more machines will come, and with them will come—are already coming—harsher laws, police in the woods, undercover agents, and the rising likelihood of violence between human beings. The real machine is not the bulldozer but the economy itself, and to fight it on its own terms, violence against violence, though understandable and even valiant, will almost certainly fail.

The second reason concerns not the immediate effectiveness of the action but its long-term effect, measured by its impact on other people. If I sabotage the bulldozer, I may feel that I have done my utmost, that I have committed myself deeply and made the most forceful statement I could make. But how will that statement be received by those who are uncommitted, those whose allegiance must be won if the movement itself is to win? Will they be moved against the violence of those who cut trees, or will they be moved against the violence of those who destroy bulldozers? Will they see the need for environmental justice, or will they see the need for harder justice against criminals?

As with the nuclear-plant occupation I took part in, I'm not sure of the answers. The radicals point out that monkeywrenching is in the American grain—the Boston Tea Party and other violences against property helped galvanize the colonists' revolutionary will. I suspect, however, that most contemporary Americans tend to associate destruction of property, no matter the motive behind it or the principles governing it, with simple vandalism. And that impression can only be bolstered by the tone of adolescent relish that pervades parts of *Ecodefense, Earth First Journal,* and some of the public statements of Earth First! members. The radicals have accused mainstream environmentalists, with some justice, of being more in love with lunching and lobbying than with saving the land. With equal justice, I believe, it can be said that the techniques and titillation of monkeywrenching have become, for some of the radicals, an end rather than a means.

If monkeywrenching is hard to gauge in terms of its public impact, there exists a different strategy with a proven record. If, instead of sabotaging the bulldozer, I and others were to stand in front of it when the catskinner came to start it, and if we weren't to move, and if when we were arrested and taken away others were to stand between the bulldozer and the grove, and others after them—eventually the dozer would probably get through, the road would probably be built and the grove cut down, but what we did in that place would save other groves. Nonviolent resistance has only one power, but that power is a great one—the inestimable power of its moral example. The black demonstrators who endured without retaliation the insults and blows and jails of enraged Southern whites moved a nation. Their dignity and courage were impossible to ignore, and when the environmental movement summons the same kind of dignity and courage, it too will be impossible to ignore. Dave Foreman, cofounder of Earth First!, showed the way in 1983 on Bald Mountain Road in southern Oregon, when he stood in front of a moving construction truck, grabbed the bumper when the truck hit him, and hung on with his knees being knocked and torn for a hundred yards until the truck stopped. In that one act, I believe, Earth First! accomplished more than it ever can with all the nails and grinding compound in the world.

And it showed how radical and conventional environmentalists can work together. Foreman's blockade, and others that followed, held off the road builders and loggers long enough, and brought enough public attention to the issue that the Oregon Natural Resources Council was able to raise money and obtain an injunction. Bald Mountain Road, though slightly extended, has never been completed, and the old-growth forest it is aimed at remains substantially intact. As well as producing the standard effect of radicalism—namely, making the demands of the moderates more palatable by comparison—Earth First! and similar groups are sometimes able to save, through their quick and bold actions, places and lives that might be lost before mainstream organizations can mobilize.

The struggle for an environmentally responsible society is a large, complicated, and immensely difficult job. It is very possibly too large and too difficult to be accomplished. But racial injustice and violence also seemed an insoluble problem, until the dreams of many people and groups of people found forms of action that made change happen—incomplete change, always in peril of dissolving, but real change nonetheless. It's possible that environmentalism might succeed in the same way, and success is more likely if we recognize that all of us are pursuing a single work through a necessary variety of means. Diversity, in human movements as in natural systems, is a sign of health. The wealthy Republican in Palo Alto who gives four-figure sums to the Wilderness Society donates for those who can't give money, and the Earth Firster who stands in the bulldozer's path stands for us all. No human mind can encompass the whole truth, and no single effort will open the way to success. If each of us takes up a share of the work, and if all of us pursue it as thoughtfully and thoroughly as we can, the work has a chance.

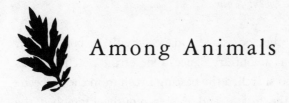

Among Animals

THE RACCOONS HAVE MADE our front porch a stop on their nightly circuit. Sometime after dark, often very late, one or two will come rustling out of the undergrowth, pausing here and there to acquaint themselves with a smell or to scratch the leaf-covered ground, making their leisured way to the light of the living room window. If there's cat food to be had, they have it, crouching at the bowl, lifting the kibble dexterously with their slender front paws. Occasionally one will stand on hind legs and peer at the floor-to-ceiling window, which surely blares an intense brightness to the coon's night eyes. My wife and I must appear as mysterious hulking silhouettes, without visual texture or scent. Once, when my wife's children were visiting, they played a hand game with two yearling coons. Boys and coons faced each other through the window, paws to the glass, and where a kid's paw went a coon's paw followed, quickly and slowly, the young of separate species doing a dance known to both at the boundary between their worlds.

On another occasion, I danced with a coon myself, though it was a contrary dance. One of the porch regulars leaned up and snatched the basting brush from the barbecue —she had the bristle end in her mouth, I grabbed the handle, and we had a tug-of-war. I felt her willfulness, her lively mass. Her curled lips revealed longer and sharper and more plentiful teeth than an animal known for its cuteness ought to possess, and much closer to my bare hand than was comfortable. When the brush slipped from her jaws she slid back from the force of her pulling, then lumbered forward, intent on that tasty wad of bristles. I offered and we danced again, a fresh prickly energy traveling my arm.

Something in that encounter refreshed me deeply. I take nourishment in seeing a deer in the field or hearing an owl in the night woods, a nourishment that comes no other way. For a moment, it completes my living nature. Enchantment, curiosity, mystery, recognition, awe—they all form part of what I feel. It's an appreciation of the animal's beauty, the miracle of its physical perfection, but of something more as well, something Denise Levertov gets at in a poem: "What is this joy? That no animal / falters, but knows what it must do?" The ant traversing the window sill, the raccoon stepping slowly through underbrush, the Arctic tern flying from pole to pole, they do not falter. They pursue their ancient ways, they enact the intelligent customs of their various kinds. This has been called mere instinct. I call it dignity and grace.

One spring I saw a coyote in a field across the road from Stanford Medical Center. He was hunting gophers— creeping up, tensing, launching himself lightly in a high arcing pounce. The gophers were everywhere, spraying up dirt like little ground-geysers, popping out of their holes and popping back in. The coyote was in the midst of plenty, and he was having fun. So were we onlookers across the road, doctors and patients, white-coated technicians, janitors and passersby. Even some of the glossy cars driving past slowed and pulled over. Coyotes are heard and sometimes seen in the Peninsula hills but rarely sound or show themselves on the Palo Alto flats. I found myself chatting with strangers. We murmured happily at the coyote's agile play, approving when he snagged a gopher and shook it quickly in his mouth like a bit of rag.

That coyote was a novelty to us, and in one sense he was absurdly out of place. His field of plenty was a small oasis in a world of cars, buildings, and packed people. But he was there all the same, and though the gophers would have disagreed, anyone watching could see that he was occupying his rightful place. He belonged there. And isn't that what pleases us so deeply? The wild animal lives in unbroken membership, part of the land in ways we humans lost, or mostly lost, a long time ago. Land for us has become a platform for our busyness, an inconvenience to travel across, a scenic backdrop to our work and recreation. As we develop concern for its health, it becomes "the environment"—still distanced and largely abstract, something around us, not something we are in. The coyote in the field has no "environment." He is at home. For many of us there is joy in that, and for some of us a pang.

Not everyone feels either joy or pang. "There are some who can live without wild things, and some who cannot," wrote Aldo Leopold, who could not. In end-of-the-twentieth-century America we have so removed our lives from the wild, so bundled ourselves in the mantle of human things and concerns, that many of us can scarcely see wild animals when we do encounter them. Once in Stanford's inner quad I was watching a great horned owl on the roof of the English building. A pair of the owls used to nest in the quad's palm trees, and they were often visible, sometimes calling back and forth, in the early evening. A woman I knew slightly, a graduate student in Modern Thought and Literature, inquired what I was looking at. I told her. She stared a while, and eventually in all earnestness she asked, "Is that really an owl, or is it a kid in an owl suit?"

For days thereafter I tried to see my colleagues and students not as people but as animals in people suits. It was hard to do. We were sitting in people rooms in people buildings, talking about people and the lives and work of people. It was a people realm we were in; comfortably enclosed, we fit there. The owl didn't, and so the graduate student didn't believe her eyes. More and more of us grow up never seeing wild animals except on TV, where they don't exist, and in zoos, where they exist displaced and displayed, and thus inevitably have an air of irreality. They are turned into visual objects, set off behind railings, framed in their cages and enclosures. The coyote in the teeming field is not a coyote when placed in a pen. He does not belong there. Among animals, only we humans create cages for ourselves and seem to thrive.

The closest I've been to a big wild animal was years ago in the Yosemite high country. My friend and I, hiking back to the valley after an aborted climb, left our packs where we intended to camp and walked to the valley rim to enjoy the evening light. When we came back, a fat black bear was raking through the packs, sitting comfortably on the ground as if she owned it. She had already scattered sleeping bags and climbing gear and was now getting into our food. We yelled and threw pinecones. She glanced her narrow eyes in our direction and went back to work, chomping intently on a freeze-dried dinner. She had a cub with her, so we didn't press the issue. Not that we could have discouraged her anyway. She was doing exactly what she wanted to do. She was willful, she was wild, and there was no dancing with her. All our possessions, edible or not, seemed to interest her passionately. She snuffled into stuff sacks, flung pots and tennis shoes, and took at least one bite into every plastic water bottle we had with us, as well as two tin cans of chicken, before plodding off into the trees.

Besides that bear, I haven't seen many animals in the backcountry. Friends of mine have stared into the eyes of mountain lions, badgers, bobcats, bighorn sheep—I see chipmunks, and once in a while a deer. I console myself, though I know it's a terrible kind of consolation, that nobody sees many wild animals now because there aren't many. Lewis and Clark, crossing the Dakota plains in 1805, entered a country "covered with herds of Buffaloe, Elk & Antelopes," the animals "so gentle that we pass near them while feeding, without appearing to excite any alarm among them. . . . They frequently approach us more nearly to discover what we are, and in some instances pursue us a considerable distance apparently with that view."

Animals—the nonhuman kind, at least—have learned a few things in the two hundred years since Meriwether Lewis wrote. They have discovered what we are. Something like the friendly intermingling that Lewis experienced may still be possible in Alaska and northern Canada. I don't know. I do know that the last time I saw buffalo was through a wire fence in middle Tennessee, a small reintroduced herd on a range where the native population had long since been exterminated. They drifted with their grazing, decidedly uninterested in me. And as for antelope, I know them best by their vibrant white rumps disappearing just as fast as their legs can hurry them.

We live among traces of an animal abundance that now seems almost unimaginable. Sixty million buffalo, maybe a hundred million, ranged from Pennsylvania to the Rockies, Georgia to Hudson Bay. Passenger pigeons swarmed in flights of over a billion birds, darkening the sky for hours, for days sometimes, making even at distance a noise that Audubon likened to a hard gale at sea. When they lighted in the hardwood forests, they broke down large limbs and left the ground covered three inches deep in dung. William Bartram, who may have embellished his account but may not have, saw Florida's St. Johns River packed solid with bellowing alligators gorging on a seasonal fish run, surging out of the water with jaws full of flapping tails, blood streaming, their nostrils jetting spumes of vapor.

At another point in his *Travels,* Bartram's reflections on a turtle dinner suggest—poignantly, two centuries later —both the original abundance of North America and the human ways, as innocent as they were greedy, that would devastate it. "We had a large and fat one served up for our supper," he writes,

> which I at first apprehended we had made a very extravagant waste of, not being able to consume one half of its flesh, though excellently well cooked: my companions, however, seemed regardless, being in the midst of plenty and variety, at any time within our reach, and to be obtained with little or no trouble or fatigue.

We came into the midst of plenty with no ethic, and no sense of the need for one, to govern our use of it. And so we live in a plenty of ourselves and our works, multiplying freely over a diminished land. Since Columbus stepped onto the shore of San Salvador five centuries ago, more than a hundred kinds of vertebrate animals alone have been exterminated in North America. Three hundred and sixty animal species or subspecies are currently listed as endangered or threatened under the Endangered Species Act. Over sixteen hundred others are candidates for listing; the law can't keep up. The holocaust in the rainforests receives more attention, but we in America are contributing directly and substantially in our own home to the global mass extinction now underway. The animals we have lost and are losing here are just as irretrievable as those in the tropics, and we are the reason they are disappearing. They were part of the land before we came, for ages before we came, and many of them will never be part of it again: passenger pigeon, California grizzly, Carolina parakeet, dusky seaside sparrow, Atlantic gray whale, eastern elk, blue pike, eleven subspecies of wolves, Wisconsin cougar, heath hen, sea mink, great auk . . .

I like to walk the driveway at night. With my eyes at ease, freed of the daytime complexity of light and shadow, leaves and branches, birds to follow, my hearing opens out. This is the hill we barrel up and down in our cars, blowing a stormwind through the boughs, occasionally glimpsing a pair of eyes or vanishing tail. We miss a lot. It's good to walk here slowly, to sit a while on the warm pavement, listening to the life of the oak forest. A rustling now and then. Soft scrape of branches. Tree crickets pulsing steady.

At a slight sound overhead I flick my light on, and I'm staring at the calm huge eyes of a small screech owl. I rise slowly, until my eyes are almost level with his. He bobs, hops to one side on his branch, as if trying to get a better look at me. I shift the light beam; his black pupils shrink in their enormous yellow fields. The light must blind him, yet he seems composed, curious. If he couldn't see, why would he stay? He hops to a lower branch, still looking at me. Or at something.

He's all eyes, this owl. His body is a slight feathered missile to fly those orbs through dark. They are spacious windows to his owl soul. What do they show? Not fear. Not pride, either, nor confidence, though it's tempting to *think* those feelings there. His eyes seem filled with lively interest. Or is that just me? But look at how he shifts and tilts, sharpening his fix on whatever of my being he sees. A mothlike stir of wings, and he's gone. *Awareness,* I'm thinking. It's the face of awareness itself.

I had the same feeling some years ago when four or five screech owls—I really can't say how many—lit in the oak one evening as I walked the trail from the cottage. For a few seconds the tree was alive with little owls looking at me, bobbing and shifting, uttering small cries. It was one of the most astonishing experiences of my life. I felt visited with blessing. And I felt kindred minds around me.

I know that many biologists would not agree that an owl is a conscious being. The possibility that animals might possess awareness and thought has long been out of fashion in our culture. Under the sway of behavioral psychology, and the older biases of Descartes and the eighteenth-century rationalists, most scientists and most of the rest of us have tended to view animals as bundles of automatic responses, driven by the determinism of genetic programing. That isn't what the screech owl's eyes told mine, and it doesn't make much sense in any case. The owl and I have evolved on the same planet for three and a half billion years, and only recently in that range of time have we taken separate paths. Why would it happen that my brain became a seat of thought and consciousness, and not the owl's? My own awareness is all bound up with my senses. When they're not being blasted with a flashlight, the owl's eyes are a hundred times more sensitive than mine. He can hear a mouse running on bare ground a hundred feet away. Those miracles of perception, and not a thinking mind?

The biologist Donald Griffin has written two books, *The Question of Animal Awareness* and *Animal Thinking,* advancing the modest claim that certain animal behavior can be better explained by assuming consciousness and thought rather than simple stimulus-response—and not just the behavior of "higher" animals. A honeybee, with a brain the size of a grass seed, can communicate through dance the distance, direction, and relative desirability of a newly found patch of flowers. One phase of her dance is a straight run on a vertical surface in the hive, during which she vigorously waggles her abdomen. The duration of this run indicates distance, and the intensity of her waggling expresses desirability. But most remarkable is her symbolic communication of direction: her dance line varies from the vertical as the flower direction varies from the sun. Pretty sophisticated behavior for an instinct-bound automaton.

Darwin, well over a century ago, recognized not only our physical kinship with other animals but a continuity between our mental lives as well. We still find it hard to swallow—and why, I wonder? Why is it so threatening to acknowledge that we're fundamentally no different from other animals? Why do we need so badly to see ourselves as a special case? We're remarkable enough. It's unlikely that another species is capable of our range and acuity of thought. Honeybees may think, but they probably don't think about whether or not *we* think. And what if they did? Would it be such a blow? And how will we ever find out *what* they think if we view them as little winged robots?

Personally, I used to draw the line at ants. Coons and owls and coyotes might think, honeybees might communicate symbolically, but the little black ants that march all summer in steady columns up and down our wisteria vines

—they're so drearily mechanical, so rigidly directed, it's easy to think of them as mindless. But in Donald Griffin's books I learn of the lives of other kinds of ants, ants that tend huge fungus farms, ants that recruit their sisters for warfare with one kind of gesture and for food gathering with another, ants that use sponges of leaf or wood to carry ten times more food than they could carry in their stomachs. So who's to say about my little black ants? If a researcher from Antares looked at the Bayshore Freeway, or at downtown San Francisco, or any town or city or highway in the world, he might infer that humans are as rigidly and mindlessly driven as it seems to me these ants are. We know we're not. What do the ants know?

On a ten-thousand-foot mountaintop in southern Arizona, work has begun on a $200 million observatory that will aim three powerful new telescopes at the galaxies and nebulas of distant space. If some environmentalists have their way, the observatory won't be completed. Their concerns are closer to the ground than those of the scientists and institutions backing the project. Building the observatory will require the partial destruction of Mount Graham's old-growth forest of spruce and fir. That forest is a unique island ecosystem in a desert region; animal species don't migrate between Mount Graham and other mountain systems. One native animal, the Mount Graham red squirrel, is recognized as an endangered subspecies whose population probably numbers fewer than two hundred. With its forest habitat disrupted, the squirrel may very possibly be driven to extinction.

Such conflicts between the works of man and the existence of obscure animals have become almost commonplace since passage of the Endangered Species Act. Building a large dam imperils a species of small fish. A variety of butterfly stalls the development of an industrial park. For those of us who don't much believe in the need for more dams and industrial parks, the choice in such cases is usually clear—as clear as it is for those builders and boosters who dismiss our concerns as sentimental or as mere pretext for an antitechnology, antiprogress agenda. But the case of the observatory, for me, is more difficult. I don't know a lot about astronomy, but I find it exciting. I'm fascinated by the glimpses of the universe it reveals—red giants and spiral nebulas, black holes and mysterious great walls in the far deeps of space and time. I would like to know more. A new industrial park is one more excess of our polluting growth economy. Most dams are built mainly to justify the federal agencies that build them. But a new observatory might tell us truths about the nature of the cosmos, and how it came to be, and how it might be evolving.

Should a tiny population of squirrels stand in the way? Secretary of the Interior Manuel Lujan, to his credit, has asked the question that must exist in many other minds: "Do we have to save every subspecies?" Obviously, the

Mount Graham red squirrel could disappear from its place, and from the evolutionary life of Earth, and the life of no human being would change. The squirrels are so few in number that the ecosystem of the mountain itself would change only slightly. A niche would open, to be filled by other life forms, and the natural economy of the mountain would go on, altered but viable. Species have been dying out since the planet came to life, after all. Ninety-nine percent of all species ever to inhabit Earth are extinct.

But there's a distinction to be made. To equate the consciously destructive acts of *Homo sapiens* with the workings of evolution is to beg the question. Nature proceeds by its own unintentional genius, a genius that gives rise to the lives of individuals and species, and, in its own time, requires their deaths. We did not create the Mount Graham red squirrel and place it on its mountaintop, and so it is not for us to decide that the Mount Graham red squirrel is expendable. Three and a half billion years of evolutionary intelligence have gone into the squirrel's making, as into ours, as into all the interwoven lives of Earth. If we are capable of subjecting ourselves to anything, we should subject ourselves to that intelligence. We live, necessarily, by tampering with nature. We have tampered freely and destructively on this continent for five hundred years. It is time—past time—to hold ourselves and our tampering under careful limits.

But what of the observatory, and the window on the

universe that it would open? I would like to know what it might show us. But interesting as that potential knowledge might be, the observatory in its present site epitomizes the tragic irony of our society's technical ambition and accomplishment. As our science sharpens its eyes, peering farther into remote space and deeper into the subatomic structure of matter, we see ourselves and our relationship to the rest of earthly nature with nothing close to sufficient clarity. The knowledge we most urgently need is the knowledge of how to act responsibly as living members of Earth. Science has a major role to play in finding that knowledge, but nothing in the light of remote stars, or in the minute stirrings of quarks and gluons, is going to help us. The wisdom we need, if we find it at all, we'll find here, on the common surface of this homeland that gave birth to us, and to all the life we know.

There's a Zuni oral narrative, translated by Dennis Tedlock in *Finding the Center,* about a boy who is born to a woman made pregnant by the Sun. His mother abandons him under a juniper tree, and there he is found by a doe and her two fawns. The mother deer nurses the boy; she and the fawns warm him with their furred bodies; they raise him as part of their family. But he isn't a deer. He is a daylight person, a human being. His deer mother knows that he is different and that his difference must be respected. She goes to Kachina Village for moccasins and garments to clothe him.

She knows, with the omniscience of the oracle in Greek tragedy, that the boy will be caught and reclaimed by the kinspeople who have sighted him, clothed in white, running with the herds of deer. She explains this to the boy, telling him that she and his deer siblings will be killed and taken with him to the village of the people. What she says comes to pass. The boy is restored to his human clan. He confronts his human mother and forces her to acknowledge him. But he is not at home. He wanders despondently for three days, and finally, on an errand for his mother to gather yucca for her basket making, he pulls the center blades of the yucca plant into his heart.

The boy may have intended to kill himself, or his death may have been an accident. The story doesn't say. And it doesn't need to say, because clearly he had to die. Having been raised with the deer, having lived and run with the deer in the open land, he could never belong to the human world. He was a daylight person, he had to return to his human kin, and when he did he was lost. He was a stranger wherever he walked, bearing a loneliness impossible to heal.

The full burden of his despair I can't imagine, but there are times when I feel traces of something like his loneliness, a loneliness not for human beings. When the screech owls filled the oak outside my door, uttering their calls, holding me in their yellow eyes and the bright clarity of their minds, and were gone—I felt it then. And I felt it once as I watched from a distance two black bears climbing a mountain gorge, making their leisurely stiff-legged way among pools and boulders, ranging higher and higher into that wilderness where I couldn't follow, where I rightly had no place. And I felt it when I listened in the high desert dark to coyotes giving up the ecstatic ghost of their song, close by somewhere in the chilly night but infinitely far from where I stood, shivering with a song for which I had no voice, their cries burning in the darkness like a fire I couldn't find.

We of the modern world have been leaving the family of animals for a long time. I suppose we were already leaving millions of years ago on the African plains when we first took tools and weapons in our hands, and later when we first spoke words among ourselves. All the time as we settled the world we were withdrawing from it. We were building human worlds with their own kinds of wonder, becoming farmers and merchants, inventors and thinkers, makers of cities and wagers of war. But we were leaving slowly. There was much we still shared with animals until a time not long ago at all—until our machines took fire and grew magically powerful, until our roads and constructions sprawled across the land, channeling and closing us in, until we grew and spread in such vast numbers that now wherever we turn we see ourselves. With our peculiar obsessive genius we carve the land to accommodate our human ways, and the animals that can't accommodate us are shrinking back, they fade to the last wild places, they disappear.

We have done and made great things on our aberrant

road, but the cost has also been great, to us as well as to other lives. Having stripped ourselves of the kinship of fellow creatures, we are alone like no other animal on Earth. We stand on the lofty peak of our human achievement, proud of our superiority, the scope of our view unparalleled in all of sentient nature—and everything else that lives is far below, in the common valleys we have left behind. There is nothing but ourselves in the clear bright air of our accomplishment. We are not alone, of course. We have our own company, we have language and what remains of our traditions, we have our homes and roads and cities, we have the artificial environment of energy and things we fabricate from the raw materials of the planet. It is not a mountaintop we inhabit but a resplendent tower of our own construction, strong and seamless, built with windows to view the scenery, rising higher and higher out of the ground of earthly life.

Many are perfectly content, even delighted, to live in the tower, and they imagine our kind can live there forever. But even if we could, for some of us a world enclosed by human beings and human things is not enough. We'll never again be members of the land as other animals are. We are daylight people, we live by the artifice of our kind. But we are animals too, born into a world of animals. We share the same sun, the same wind and rain, grass and trees, the same hospitable surface of this planet that became alive. Separate and together, we are born of mystery into mystery, expres-

128

sions of a single miracle. It lives in the raccoon's quick paws and lively strength, in the bear's glance and the red squirrel gripping the limb, in the cries of the coyote, the gaze of the deer, the honeybee's dance. It swims in rivers and sea, flies on wings through the ocean of air, it stirs in the stillness of the forest night—it burns in the screech owl and it burns in me, the same fire, the same brief fire, shining from eyes to other eyes.

Desert Walking

MY FRIEND JOHN, whom I've known
since childhood, entered a Vedic monastic order after college and spent ten years as a renunciate monk in southern
California, cut off from his former life and the outside
world. In those years he studied rigorously and meditated
four to five hours a day. When he decided to emerge from
isolation, he bought a four-wheel-drive pickup and started
traveling to desert places in California and Arizona. He
camped and hiked, usually alone, for days and sometimes
weeks at a time. It was in the desert that he felt closest to
the mystery of being. The created universe, as I understand
his belief, is in reality a vibration, a single tone struck in
the beginning from Spirit. Alone in the quiet of stone and
sand, my friend listens for the sound of all that is.

John and I argue when we see each other. We have
never hiked together in the desert, possibly never will—
there's a good chance we would drive each other crazy. But
I listen to him. There's much in his religion that seems
strange to me, but I respect his search, I respect his disci-

131

pline, and I understand him when he talks about the desert. I too keep going there. Something in its silences keeps calling me. I see a little farther there. Religion is from *religare,* to tie back. Walking freely in desert emptiness, I learn a little more of what it is that I am tied to.

*

The lowering sun still much too hot, my neck and arms already burned, I wondered why I had driven eight hundred miles for this. I had done a lot of backpacking but all in mountains, Sierra Nevada and Oregon Cascades, among lakes and flowery high meadows, in conifer woods as comfortable as old clothes. This was different. This was glaring knife-edged boulders strewn down barren slopes, clumps of wizened and eaten prickly pear, a scattering of stunted pines. This was the rank green scummy pool by which I'd dropped my pack, miserably heavy with five gallons of city water, and now sat panting in disgust, waiting for the sun to dive behind the Panamint crest.

The beautiful is a dangerous idea. Once inside it, it's hard to see out. I knew the High Sierra was beautiful, with its tumbling runnels and glacial brilliance and green expanses—but this oven of a desert gorge? This stark prison I had worked so hard to enter, scattering lizards, chucking rocks at the braying goomered burro who'd stood in my way? It was like spending years reading Wordsworth, page after lovely page, and suddenly hitting William Carlos

Williams. Is this *poetry?* These fractured lines, these bare *things,* unadorned in the rhetoric of green?

But the place was working on me, of course, even as I sat there. Even in my sunburned weariness I felt its freshness. By sundown I was admiring how pinyon roots jam tight in rock crevices, how their stiff limbs creak in a rise of wind. The land's red and yellow mineral streakings glowed in the last light. Death Valley cooled in pale haze below me. Two frogs started to chirp at dusk—they liked the place just fine, and kept telling me. A cool wash of moonlight, the stones radiant with hoarded warmth, a little wind at work. And next morning, as I hiked on, the canyon took me in. Narrowing, it played a slow winding rhythm between sheer walls, each turn a gateway to the unknown. I climbed dry waterfalls, clattered across loose gravel, slogged through sand and kept on walking, winding in and out of light and shadow, breeze and stillness, following the scent of sun-warm stone and the bright piping of a bird I never saw.

*

Driving Highway 140 southeast from the Warner Mountains in Oregon, you pass from pine forest down into Deep Creek Canyon, where the slopes are studded with the squat green flame-shapes of junipers. The canyon dumps you out into open basin and range, a few trees fringing the higher ground. They grow sparser as you drive on, deeper into the

Great Basin, until topping out on Doherty Rim you see a wind-beaten clump on the left, and way off to the right there's a single flat-crowned juniper—the final tree.

Somehow, by bird or rat or stormwind, a seed arrived in the right place at the right time. In a crevice among lichen-crusted scabrocks, possibly shaded by a clump of sage, it found just enough moisture for just enough time to elaborate its roots and begin to rise, imperceptibly through the seasons, alone in a high dryland sea. Beyond that tree, except for the planted poplars of an occasional ranch, it's nothing but small sage and rabbitbrush, crumbling crops of volcanic rock, nothing but the long contours of the open land, all the many miles to the Pine Forest Mountains of Nevada.

Desert presents itself in particularities. Thirty miles across wavering flats, Shiprock stands in stillness. A coyote lopes along a ridge and disappears. Deep in a canyon, one cottonwood flares yellow against pink stone. A silvery luminescence next to my foot takes shape as *frog* on gray limestone. Above me on a ledge, one clump of cactus has unfurled its papery burgundy flowers. A raven croaks—part of me waits all day to hear it again. The parched hillside I've been climbing reveals a small band of aspens huddled in a crease of land where a clear spring rises.

The eye moves from point to point, thing to particular thing, great and small. The mind can take its time, surrounding what it wonders at without distraction, and each object takes on heightened life. Maybe that's why my own life feels heightened in the desert. I too am here, a singularity myself, as improbably rightful as the one juniper, the clear spring, the sundown glow that flares the canyon walls and dies away.

*

As I walk up a canyon, I move toward source and seeing. Each twisting turn, each dry chute I climb opens the way a little farther. When the canyon forks, I hesitate. I have to choose one way. On steep sections my hands and feet work in concert—I have purpose, I am focused ahead, I ascend as if toward an astonishing secret at the canyon's origin. If I'm allowed to climb far and high enough, the walls that have been confining me may lower themselves. The sky broadens, surrounding me slowly, openness on my shoulders. I see the canyon that led me here winding away below. I see parts of neighboring canyons, spires of stone, buttes and mesas, blue mountains ranging away on the world's curve. The secret may be the rock I'm sitting on. Or it may be out there somewhere, in the complication of the carved land.

As I walk down a canyon, the tendency of the entire land collects me. I was alone on the dry flat where I started, but as little walls channel the sandy wash, company appears. Bunchgrass may be the first. A single flower shouts blue. The sand is damp, and after a while water is trickling beside me, sloshing around my boots, and the walls have shouldered higher. Willows trail their limbs in the current. Cottonwoods tremble to a breeze I can't feel. Swallows chitter overhead, where the blue sky has been squeezed thin by stone expanses only the sun can climb. Along their base, other humans left markings long ago. Like me, like the grasses and the willows, the swallows and the cottonwoods, they followed the voice of steady changefulness, the fluent voice that says, *I am the one who sings through stone. I called you here. I know the way.*

*

Brown boulders the size of houses choke the mouth of a side canyon, jagged-edged, lighter-colored where they split away, not long ago, from the upper walls. A forty-foot spire has sheared from the wall and dropped straight down, implanting itself among the riverbank cottonwoods whose contortions bear witness to brutal floods. Titanic violence composes this serenity I come for. These monolithic walls are splitting, sliding, crumbling to sand. The canyon is scouring deeper. I miss a lot, visiting for a dot of time, a week, a human life.

Any wilderness speaks silently of time, but time is nowhere clearer than in desert canyons. Descending millions of years through solid sand dunes, red mud mires, the rippled bottoms of ancient seas, here I walk *in* time, dwarfed by the mute magnitude of eons. Here, along with other newcomers—wren, cottonwood, lizard—I am swallowed in the long story of Earth. I walk in a stillness like no other, and though I don't hear what John hears, the sound of all that is, I feel it close. I imagine walking deeper than I can, down to the black stone that cooled from fiery torrents when the planet's face was red and flowing. And I dream deeper still, of entering the original fire itself, where if I lost myself I might for just one instant grasp the puzzle of being, my mind in its last speck of time might ride the leaping arc from nothingness to solid worlds.

*

The answers to the biggest questions are hard to come by, even in the desert. Bruce, my frequent hiking partner, is a molecular biologist. He studies the minute workings of life, and he tells me it's very much a mystery how life became alive. It's simply unknown to the bright minds and prodigious equipment of science how nucleic acids began to replicate themselves, how the translation of RNA into proteins evolved, and how these baffling developments came to be incorporated within a cell membrane. Once you have the cell, says Bruce, it's not *too* hard—though it took another two billion years—to get to the elaboration of complex life forms. Once you have the cell.

The startling fact is that a rock-and-water planet came to life. Nothing is more apparent, and nothing is less understood. Unlike many of his colleagues, Bruce doesn't scorn the idea that life may have originated from spores that arrived in meteors. Given how little is known, he says, no plausible theory can be dismissed. He will entertain any explanation within the bounds of nature, any explanation short of God. Bruce is a scientist. He doesn't care much for religion.

"But what if God is nothing outside nature," I'm arguing tonight. "What if God is in nature, *is* nature, and evolution is God's way of being born?"

"Why do you have to call it God?" he says. "Listen. Matter is so subtle and so incredibly complex it doesn't *need* to be dressed up with divinity."

I can't refute that. I'm not sure I want to refute it. We look at the fire, drinking our brandy, and after a while I wander off to my sleeping bag. Staring at the brink of cliff straight overhead, silhouetted against stars, I'm unsettled. *Nothing, something. No-life, life.* We're looking at the same thing, neither of us can explain it, and we make different leaps of faith. Being is so extraordinary he doesn't need to call it divine. Being is so extraordinary I can only call it divine. We see contrariwise and we see the same. What we see, we love.

The bumpy shadows on the cliff brink are bothering me. I'm worried that one of the less subtle acts of matter might flatten me in the night, and so I drag my sleeping bag farther under the overhang, a little closer to the fire, a little closer to where Bruce is sleeping. Tomorrow we'll talk more. We'll walk on up the canyon, and we'll both keep our eyes open.

*

This heat is *palpable,* it's pressing solid, almost seems to hold me upright as I lurch and stumble with my load. I'm not hot, I'm *wired,* I'm dancing with the bees around pink cactus blooms, the stones a bright dry river passing under. Somewhere along this big bajada there's a canyon mouth, there's cool rock shade, there's a place to drop this water tank I've packed for miles—a water tank myself, of course, a pouch of ancient sea traipsing on two legs through a hundred twelve degrees of blessed sun. Is this what evolution had in mind when that lungfish flopped out on the shore? Am I the avant-garde, the pioneer? I'm a fool, I'm way outside my depth, I'm stumbling like a drunkard here where stones and cactus, everything but bees holds still in heat, I'm crazy with bright clarity—those peaks across the valley close enough to touch, to drink, to swallow whole and keep on walking, as this lit vastness swallows me.

*

First it was soft hail beads, falling thickly, bouncing off the red sandstone, sliding down the angled slabs, jumping on the ground as if alive. Then papery flakes, with wind, thinning now to fine sugar specks. The silent storm fills the wash, gray and blind and steadily sifting down.

The snow terraces itself on ledges, sticks in delicate scallops on steeper surfaces. The bushy pines and junipers are frosted with it. Yuccas gather it in, each of them holding a loose ball, their straight yellow spines sticking through. Each tree and shrub, alive and dead, gracefully accepts the snow. I hear it ticking on the rocks. Water drips from the overhang. My fire flutters.

Waiting out a snowstorm under a dripping ledge is not what I expected. I had hoped to be miles farther by now, miles closer to the canyons I came to see. But the canyons will be there tomorrow. They'll be there for a long time. A destination sets you in motion, but once you're moving here, what's important is where you are. That's what I keep forgetting out there among cars and books and jobs. I forget this presentness. I need this slowing down— to open outward, to be still, to gather in what comes as the yuccas gather their globes of snow.

*

After breakfast Bruce and I eat a few mushrooms and set out to explore the little canyon where we've camped. It's a hot morning. The stream collects in several deep tanks, clear and green, and Bruce can't resist. Scientists need to relax. They lead intense lives, one eye screwed to the microscope, the other scanning for the next grant—and hoping for a glimpse of the wild Nobel. I leave him splashing, a goofy grin on his face, and continue upcanyon.

A fly drones under a tree. Ambling along, I'm clothed in the heat of the day. Nothing changes really. Rocks don't turn to jelly, visions don't boil from the sky. Mind emerges from its usual cave, infusing the body, and with all your senses you remember—*yes, this is how it is.* The tree, the droning fly, everything is only more itself. Climbing the slope of bitterbrush, I smooth my hands along the canyon wall, press my cheek to its coolness, inhale its ancient smell.

From the end of the earth will I cry unto thee, when my heart is overwhelmed: lead me to the rock that is higher than I. It's more than I can comprehend, almost more than my heart can bear, this beauty we are born to. All this earth, and we alive in it, to walk here, to touch this solid truth. . . . *Being is its own answer,* I say out loud, from somewhere. And the words ring, they sound as from a bell inside me, inside the stone I lean against. *Being is its own answer, its own answer . . .*

On up the canyon, hiking with a boy's happiness, I'm thinking about the sixties. We were kids in a new car, revving the engine, driving way too fast. But what we glimpsed was real, the realest thing we'd ever seen. I remember me and John standing in the light rain with blankets on our shoulders, shivering half the night in a field as we tried to speak our sense of sacredness, how near it was. How near. He followed the glimpse to a monastery and out again. I followed into the world and into words. We both followed to the desert, and we're still following.

Bruce catches up, refreshed and laughing. He's been watching me, amused at how my head's been rotating angle to angle as I've walked, as if I were some yellow-capped robot. Ridiculous, I tell him. I've been immersed in important thoughts, oblivious to outward things. His vision must be affected.

We stop for a small lunch, walk again, and after a few turns of canyon we arrive where we didn't know we were heading. We're standing in a pool looking up a tall water-slide cut so deeply into stone it forms a chamber, a cool grotto crossed above our heads by a slanting arch. The smooth sculpted walls rise past the arch to a crack of blue sky far above, and the green shimmer of the water we have stirred fills the chamber—wavering sheens of light alive on our bodies, our faces, around and above us, intermingling on the surfaces of stone.

*

I follow a necessity older than my conscious choice, older than my life or any life, a way worked out through ages between the tendencies of rain and rock. Where the walls lift high, I cannot leave. My freedom is to follow, my confinement my opportunity. In the light of sun, I move forward in my human way. I walk a while in the open hold of land. Wind and water, the beautiful blind carving— none of it for me, yet there's room. I'm walking, and the way is clear.

*

I used to hope for a monumental discovery in the desert. Around each canyon bend, above each dry waterfall, up the shadowy passage of a side canyon, I longed for something I had never seen—an undisturbed Indian village, the eyes of a cougar, a visible spirit. What I really longed for was a vision, a flash of knowing in whose light I would understand my life and death, and all the hieroglyphic forms of nature.

I've walked some desert miles now, and I'm beginning to think that vision is not a sudden kind of thing. Maybe it's a progress, a slow gathering of small seeings. Maybe it has to be. Walking a canyon sometimes I'll stop, vowing to look so intensely at a certain thing—a purple flower, a sandstone spire—that its entire being will come clear to me. I stare, but my mind grows weary. The flower's language is untranslatable. I could stare until I fell to bones at the base of that rock tower, and still its sheer, water-stained surface would thwart me. Maybe, as the greatest friend and lover of these canyons insisted, its meaning *is* its surface. It stands in its peculiar form, unlike any other spire in the desert, in the universe, a monument to nothing but itself.

And so I walk again. The canyon keeps on going, and ordinary wonders mark its way. A cactus grows in a dead juniper. A small dinosaur rests on a rock. Rippling water goes orange in the late sun. The canyon keeps on winding, part shadow and part sun, revealing itself before me as it closes behind. What I see I touch with my awareness, the only light I have, and enough. I walk. And a good place to end my walk is the impassable overhang that finally blocks my way, to lie curled in its cool shade with the few ferns that live there, listening to a slow drip of water. The way I came, the way I will return, is waiting when I'm ready. And winding on above me is the canyon I will never climb, winding deep among the bluffs and spires, winding on through distant ranges, through the wilderness of scattered stars.

*

Here, where I come to get away from people, there are people who come with me. They travel the canyons too, their faces drifting in and out of my awareness—my wife, my mother and my brother, Bruce the scientist, John with his gray head listening, all my closest friends. As my mind quiets here, I see them lit with a certain still clarity, and I sense that all of us are living a forgotten story, acting perfectly ourselves, as perfectly as the stones are stones, as perfectly as the water flows. The story is close around me here, and it's never closer than in fall, when the cottonwoods turn yellow-gold against the red rock walls.

The story those trees tell is the same story sunset tells, the glad and fearful story, the story I'm alive to learn. Sunset tells it grander—you can see how vast and old it is, how other stories all form part of it, all end in that rich light. But you can't touch the sunset. You can't stand next to it or lean against it. With their trunks and limbs, their leaves that stir in the least of winds, cottonwoods bring the story down from sky and place it here, close to us, in ground.

There are graceful ones that rise in a few gentle curves of trunk. There are those with two trunks, or three, or four. There are trees that circle upon themselves in corkscrew loops. There are bowed and twisted trees, trees that wander along the ground like blind beggars, trees that dive down into sand and lift upward again. And there is one tree I've seen that grows sideways out of a silt shelf and arches back above the shelf to bury its broken crown at the bottom of the canyon wall. Its crumbling bark exposes cracked and riddled grain, and for part of its contorted length the tree is split clear open, filled with stones and dead leaves caught from the crushing floods. Along its great body it still raises a few living limbs, small trees themselves, flagged with the bright leaves of its kind.

If we didn't hide our histories inside us, we'd see our own lives as we see the trees. We'd see how some of us rise true and easily, how some are bent or split from their beginnings. We'd see where we were chafed or broken, where love failed or never was, where love returned. We'd see where troubles beset us, how we bent and twisted beneath their weight, how we've grown as we've been able to grow and never have stopped growing, branching from the single source, how in our bodies' heaviness we touch the air and tremble—how each of us, in one peculiar unlikely way, rises in the light.

Marks on the Land

A ROCKY TRAIL leads down from the Utah tableland to the winding sandy bottom of the canyon. Most rock art is easy to miss. The Great Gallery is impossible to miss. The paintings fill an alcove over a hundred feet long, and many of the figures are life-size or larger, long forms tapering downward, the color of dried blood. All head and elongated torso, no arms or legs, they seem to hover on the chalky pink sandstone as if keeping a vigil through the hundreds and probably thousands of years since they came into being. Some of the torsos are solid red, some are lined and dotted and etched in complex patterns. One of them has two small animals facing each other on its front, another has an animal on each square shoulder. Each of the forty or so major figures is different, each a nuanced variation of the stretched-escutcheon body form that the artists needed to render again and again.

At the left end of the panel, five of the solid red forms without facial features surround like shrouded attendants the largest and most distinctive figure of all. Its lower torso was only lightly shaded in with the hematite pigment and then smeared to blend with the pink stone, giving a much vaguer sense of body than in the others. The upper torso is more distinctly formed, outlined and filled with blurred horizontal striations, a set of sharp vertical lines running down the center. The wide shoulders flare slightly upward, just above the head level of the surrounding five, and its own crown-shaped head cocks back a little, the huge white outlined eyes staring up across the canyon and far away.

The figures are anthropomorphic, but it's immediately clear that they aren't human. A pair of them, with ghostly pecked-out eyes, hover above a group of small prancing bighorn sheep and two men, their legs bent and torsos flexed, who seem to dance around a stick they hold vertically between them. Or maybe they're fighting. But in either case they're clearly human beings, fluid, lively, and small. The gods hover above them and to one side, still and monolithic. It's possible that this part of the panel had to do with hunting magic. No one knows or will know exactly what these images meant to the people who created them. But even across thousands of years and an equally vast cultural gulf, one thing is clear. A religious imagination expressed itself here, working out an image of the sacred. In blood-red paint on stone, a people's sense of divinity found form.

Few other rock art images I have seen have the sheer spiritual power of the Great Gallery, but the people who study this art seem to agree that many of the paintings and petroglyphs that abound in the American West were sacramental in origin, probably a kind of pictorial prayer. The form of a bird or snake wasn't laboriously chipped into stone merely to portray the animal, but because the animal was associated with powers of the unseen world, superhuman powers that humans needed, powers that could be invoked or somehow touched by rendering an image in the tangible world. Certain images may have been intended to remind people of the songs and stories of their oral tradition, the lore by which they comprehended the world and kept themselves alive in it, the images renewing and strengthening the sense of sacredness that inspired them. Some figures, crowded together and even superimposed, may be related to the powers of a particular sacred place and may not be art at all in our sense of something made to be looked at through time—the ceremonial creation of these images may have been their entire point, their continued existence a mere accident of the medium they were formed in.

In the lower Colorado River country there are some three hundred earth figures, or geoglyphs, made by selectively scraping away the cobbled stone surface of a desert terrace to reveal the lighter-colored sediments beneath. Some of the geoglyphs are representations of human or animal forms; some are abstract designs. Many of them are so large they can be seen more clearly from the air than from the ground, which led to a popular theory that they were made to guide the navigation of ancient astronauts. That idea tells far more about the impoverished imagination of twentieth-century Americans than it tells about the geoglyphs. Archaeologists are finding that many of the images are drawn from the creation mythologies of native peoples of the region. Like paintings and petroglyphs, they are more than mere visual images. Some of them are composed of or associated with what are thought to be dance trails, with marked stations where particular elements of a ceremony might have been performed in sequence, art and religion thus embodied together in one imaginative form.

At least one archaeologist believes that the earliest geoglyphs were made as spiritual invocations to reverse the increasingly arid climate that evolved with the end of the Pleistocene epoch. There is little evidence to confirm or deny his theory. Probably the most that can be said with certainty is that many of the geoglyphs had religious significance—their exact intended purpose, like the purpose of the Great Gallery's hovering torsos, is a mystery. But the meaning of Indian rock art is no more bound by its intended purpose than the meaning of a poem is bound by the poet's intent. A friend of mine, a young archaeologist, recently found a petroglyph panel on his family's ranch in eastern Oregon where he had grown up and where I lived for several years. At the base of a low rimrock on a juniper-studded slope he found many human stick figures inscribed in rows, their hands linked together. All of us who saw the petroglyphs had ideas about their meaning, based mostly on the striking sense of unity the panel seemed to suggest. All those ideas are almost certainly wrong, but it doesn't matter. The land is richer because of that clear and artful handiwork performed by human beings long ago. A place known to us was part of their world too, important enough that they felt the need to leave their human mark upon it. That in itself imparts a kind of sanctity, whatever the intent of those who left the marks.

And whatever its intent, all rock art by its very form and nature conveys certain information about its makers. It conveys, for instance, that its makers were careful, patient, and persevering. Petroglyphs were made by striking the darkened surface of desert-varnished rock to expose lighter-colored, unweathered rock. A single sharpened stone was used, or, for greater precision, one stone was used as a chisel and another as a hammer. In either case, producing a shapely figure or set of figures is not a trivial process. One blow of too much force can knock off an entire section of surface rock, destroying the image irreparably. Patience and care were necessary to control the small violence of stone on stone and guide it toward the artist's vision of wholeness— a vision that could arise, like that of any artist, only through practice and development over time.

Another kind of information that rock art conveys has to do with its scale and placement in its surroundings. The artists did their work not on canvas or paper but on nature itself, on the given surfaces of Earth's body. There are no frames around the images, nothing to separate the composition from its environment. Every act of this kind of art was necessarily an alteration of the land, and so the scale and position and character of the art inevitably express something of how the land was understood, and how the artist understood himself in relation to the land. Every example of Indian rock art I have seen has been small and unobtrusive in the scale of its surroundings, an adaptation to what the environment allowed rather than an attempt to transform the environment to its own design. The Great Gallery, though composed of some of the largest of rock art figures, fills its natural panel without in any way overwhelming it, and the panel itself is the base of a canyon wall many hundreds of feet high. Even the geoglyphs of the lower Colorado, some of which extend for several hundred feet, are anything but huge in the spaciousness of their desert terrace setting—in all that openness, who would inscribe a miniature? And the figures are so inconspicuously formed that it's easy to walk right over one without noticing it. Restraint and discretion, I would argue, are everywhere bespoken in Indian rock art.

I realize, of course, that where I see restraint and discretion another observer might see only the limitations of stone-age technology—with spray paint and jackhammers, the Indian artists of centuries and millennia past might have made a more pronounced and less seemly impact on their environment. But that view ignores the reverence in which nature was held by traditional native societies, an attitude very different from our own. The people who first entered North America, at least twelve thousand years ago, gave rise to many distinct cultures, and to generalize about them is hazardous, but two guiding values seem to have been shared by most or all of them: the natural world was understood as sacred, filled with divinity; and humankind was understood as only one creature among many, and not necessarily the most intelligent or powerful. Given those values, it seems to me, restraint and discretion inevitably would have been exercised in any action that left a human impact on the land.

The easy pessimism that sees behavior as only a function of available technology ignores something else as well —it ignores the question of responsibility. Different ways of understanding the natural world leave different marks upon it, and the people who make those marks, not their tools, are responsible for them. Native Americans are responsible for rock paintings and petroglyphs and geoglyphs. They are responsible for the remains of their various modest habitations, from caves in the Great Basin to teepee rings on the Plains to Anasazi cliff dwellings and ruins of cities in the Four Corners country. They are responsible for fish traps, drift fences, irrigation ditches, and other remnants of their means of subsistence. In some areas they are partially responsible for vegetation patterns, due to their practice of burning to improve game habitat. And early Indians may have been partially responsible, it's thought by some, for the extinction of large Pleistocene mammals such as the woolly mammoth.

The first Americans left those marks, and we newcomers are leaving our own. Near Canyonlands National Park there is a rock that must have been a crossroads and possibly a power spot for many cultures, for its face has been inscribed with at least two thousand years of petroglyphs. Peoples of the Archaic period, Basketmakers, Fremont, Pueblo, and Navajo all have contributed to the crowded field of images, some crude, some vague, some distinctive. And we have contributed too, with names, dates, graffiti, and bullet marks. The names and dates and graffiti probably have counterparts among the Indian markings—surely not every petroglyph had a sacred purpose. But the bullet marks, I would argue, are distinctively our own. Destruction of one kind or another has been our signature on the western land.

You can see it in the California desert, where dunes, canyons, and desert pavements have been so thrashed by off-road vehicles that in many places the land is more scar then clear skin, and where many of the ancient geoglyphs have been marred or destroyed. You can see it all over the West in too many scraped and blasted roads through too many places where no road should be, where some prospector or government agency that didn't value the land thought the land might harbor something valuable. You can see it in the giant copper pits and coal mines of Nevada and New Mexico and Colorado and Arizona, and in the new mining boom now turning the Great Basin into heaps and holes, the heaps sprayed with cyanide to leach out gold, over half of which will be used to make jewelery. You can see it in rangeland "improved" by bulldozers dragging a massive chain between them to strip off the juniper forest, and you can see it wherever cows and sheep have turned grassland into dust and sagebrush, which in the intermountain West is most anywhere. You can see it, if they don't drag you away first, at the Nevada Nuclear Testing Site or at any of the military bombing ranges and training grounds that abound in California and the Southwest. And you can see it in the heroic concrete plug called Glen Canyon Dam, which in 1963 turned a hundred miles of the Colorado River and one of the monumental landforms of the continent into a lake for houseboats and water-skiers, drowning a slickrock wilderness whose beauties included Indian petroglyph panels up to a hundred feet in length.

Anthropomorphic figures are common in rock art, and we too have created many. Ours are of the colossal scale that characterizes many of our marks on the West, standing in perfect straight lines across flats and over mountains, each one identical to the others, continuous lengths of high-tension cable passing between them. Like the Indian anthropomorphs, these are related to the power of nature, but to a different kind of power. These are not made in humility, to connect the makers with the spiritual powers of Earth. These are made to carry away the power of rivers, extracted by dams, and the ancient power of the sun, extracted in coal mines and burned in gargantuan plants whose smoke turns the clear desert distance to haze. These towers made in our image carry the captured life of nature to distant cities—they carry it one way only, out of the land and into the widening mouth of our human craving.

Indians took from the land too. But they learned, very likely by hard experience, to take with respect, to take in humility, and to take no more than the land was capable of restoring. That, at least, was their ideal, which they practiced well enough to live twelve thousand years or more in the North American land without diminishing it. The ideal is evident in all aspects of their cultures: in their oral literatures, in their ritual practices, in their hunting and fishing and farming, and not least in the careful images they rendered on sacred land, the same land we have desacralized and reduced to a trove of uses and materials, taking what we can, surrounding ancient art with modern scars.

It isn't hard to interpret the marks we are making on the western landscape. No archaeological training is necessary to see that they show little sign of restraint or discretion, no sign of reverence or even respect, no sign of a governing ideal except that of human comfort and convenience at the land's expense. To find a healthier ideal we would do well to look back in time even as we look forward, as is our habit, to a bolder and better technological future. We would do well to look at certain red cedars on the Northwest coast, cedars bearing scars where planks were split out centuries ago, the trees growing on unharmed. And we would do well to look at junipers in western Nevada bearing similar scars where Paiute people cut out staves for shaping into bows, as many as four generations of staves taken from a single scar as new wood filled the opening. We can't sustain ourselves by splitting boards from living trees, but we can look to those trees that sustained others as signs of an ideal. We can try to understand and learn to express in our own ways the values those scarred trees signify. We can learn to read in them, and in other Native American marks on the land, not a simplicity we have outgrown but a necessary complexity we have not yet achieved.

157

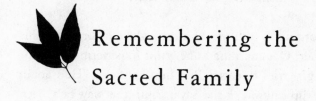

Remembering the
Sacred Family

THE MILKY LIGHT returns. It comes imperceptibly into the openness of the field. Imperceptibly, in stillness, the trunks and limbs of the oaks begin to define themselves, to emerge from the vagueness of shadow into their curving distinction. Certain birds know the change before I do—their restrained, almost solemn chirping is what wakens me, and looking out the bedroom window, I see the light is on its way.

It comes every morning, this miracle, and I rarely see it. Usually I sleep well past dawn; when I go outside the light has already arrived, complete and unremarkable. I go about my business, noticing from time to time the warmth or the cold, the brightness or lack of it, but by and large as unconscious of the solar radiance I move through as of the ground I walk on. The sun is something I assume. It happens outside my being, with my awareness or without.

Recently, though, I read about a man with a very different view of the sun. In a Zuni story translated by Dennis Tedlock, a medicine man named Payatamu goes out every morning to a shrine on a rock where he brings up his Sun Father. One morning as he walks to perform his ritual, a witch girl tries to entice him into her field. "He's going to come up anyway," she says, "just the way he's been coming up." Payatamu replies, "No, it's because of me that he comes up."

Out of context, his remark may be taken as anthropocentric arrogance—the sun is subservient to human will. But that is not Payatamu's meaning. He goes to bring up his Father not with a sense of self-importance but in a spirit of duty and humility. He goes every morning. This particular day he wavers, however, and he and the girl agree to play a high-stakes game of hide-and-seek, the loser to die at the winner's hands. Payatamu sprinkles a cornmeal road and follows it up to his Sun Father, but the girl finds him and cuts off his head. The Sun says, "I must go in at once, for I've been coming up because of you." The ritual practice is broken, and disaster falls. The world lies dark.

Our own culture tends to dismiss such ritual as based on a primitive understanding of life. But in fact it is primitive only in the sense of *primary*—of or connected to first things. Payatamu, in his ritual of dawn, takes part in a primary reciprocal relationship with the sun. He and his people are dependent on its light and warmth. The corn they grow, the deer they hunt, they themselves cannot exist without it. Mysteriously, it fills their human needs, and so Payatamu does his part to keep it rising. He believes that

160

its beneficence occurs because human beings, through proper thoughts and words and practices, approach it with humility and reverence. In short, he does not take the sun for granted. Until the morning of his fatal wavering, he takes responsibility for the sunrise.

We, in our reasonable way, take no such responsibility. Like the girl in the story, we think the sun is going to come up anyway. We understand the recurrence of light and dark to be a mechanical regularity of the planet's rotation. Nature goes on, we assume, regardless of our attention or inattention. And we go a step further. Consciously or unconsciously, we assume that nature will go on even if we actively abuse it, forcibly extracting its "raw materials" and pouring into it the poisonous waste products of our industrial civilization. We have inflicted this assumption on North America for four centuries now, justifying it in the name of such values as comfort and progress. We have created and sustained what we like to call a high standard of living. But the environmental dysfunctions we have caused and contributed to provide ample evidence, if evidence did not exist before, that it is our own understanding of life that is primitive, in the sense of crude or naive.

There is nothing naive about the message of the story of Payatamu: a human falters in his responsibility to the nature that sustains him, and as a result he dies and the world is threatened. That story is a culture's way of reminding itself—through its oral tradition, one generation to the next—of a truth it can't afford to forget. Our own European cultures must once have carried similar stories with similar themes, but we have for the most part left those stories behind, along with our sense of responsibility. The truths they once told have dissipated to bland generalities without force to guide our lives—"You can't fool Mother Nature," for instance—and have been bastardized to such purposes as selling margarine on television. We Americans, like other industrialized peoples, appreciate the natural world, but what we appreciate is not our interconnection with it. We tend to value it with a sentimental aestheticism, as something beautiful or peaceful or magnificent, or with the residual pride of our frontier experience, as the formidable foe against which we struggled and prevailed.

As we subdued the continent with our technological genius and burgeoning numbers, cautionary voices were raised by observers who saw in nature not just beauty or fearsomeness but also our kinship with it. The writings of Henry David Thoreau, George Perkins Marsh, and John Muir aroused an ecological conscience that helped bring to birth the modern conservation movement. From the beginning, however, the character of that movement has been minority and reactive. It has necessarily fought rear-guard campaigns against the excesses of our exploitive civilization, trying to save this stretch of wild river and that threatened forest, and more recently, trying to hold air and water pollution within certain limits. Conservation has not set our society's agenda; it has had all it could do to defend against it.

In the twentieth century, one conservation writer above all others tried to give the movement a broad philosophical view and a positive vision of what it needed to achieve beyond its reactive skirmishing. Aldo Leopold, writing fifty years ago, argued that humanity's expanding ethical concern needed one further expansion. We have advanced from the day when humans could own other humans as property, he noted, but land—which in Leopold's usage includes the entire biota—is still considered mere chattel, affording its owner privileges but entailing no obligations. The next step in the evolution of ethics, Leopold said, must be an ethical relationship between humans and the land. We must come to see the land as a community to which we belong, not a possession at our disposal. Calling such a land ethic "an evolutionary possibility and an ecological necessity," he believed it existed in his own time in embryo and saw mixed signs of its chances for development.

Had he lived into the sixties and seventies, Leopold would have been heartened by that period's bloom of environmental awareness and the landmark legislation that resulted. Had he lived into the eighties, he would have lost heart as he saw many of the earlier gains stalled or reversed under the Reagan administration's malign stewardship. If he were alive today, he would see America still squandering its resources—strip mines still ravaging the Appalachians, the Mississippi still carrying far too much topsoil out to sea, the western mountains being sheared of their trees at a rate he would have found unbelievable. And aside from what we are taking from the land, Leopold would have been stunned by what we are returning—toxic fumes to the sky, corrosive rain killing trees and lakes, rivers and groundwater laced with carcinogens, sludge dumps along our coasts, marshlands poisoned by agricultural runoff, and the atmosphere slowly warming around us as the overheated engine of industrial society roars on.

The chief incentive for change, Leopold hoped, would be humanity's growing awareness of its connectedness to and dependence on the natural world, as revealed by the science of ecology. And, in fact, the ideas of ecology have gained a certain currency since Leopold's time. The two Earth Days have done much to plant them in the public's mind. They are taught in schools and appear in media stories. "Our Fragile Planet" has made the cover of *Time* magazine. But for most of us, ecology remains *only* ideas, topics we read about and absorb from television and occasionally discuss at dinner. Like the sunrise, they remain effectively outside our lives, which continue, by and large, to follow the course of least resistance. We may believe in a land ethic, but we aren't living a land ethic.

It's possible that the threat of environmental calamity will scare us into changing our ways. The specters of dead forests and rising oceans and skin cancer may cause us to veer from the way of life that produces such consequences. But our tendency is to see environmental problems as either remote from where we live or remote in future time. If the trees in our neighborhood seem healthy enough, acid rain is an abstraction. As long as the greenhouse effect is a story on television or in the *New York Times,* and not an absence of bread on our tables or the presence of salt in our drinking water, it is unlikely to prompt us to use fossil fuels twice as efficiently as we now do—the order of change necessary, some scientists are saying, to mitigate global warming. We economized for a short time in the seventies, but only because gasoline wasn't in the pumps. When it returned, so did our profligate energy habits.

Industrial civilization is sustained by a powerful inertia. Businesspeople tend not to abandon practices that bring profit. Consumers tend not to repudiate the comforts, conveniences, and spendthrift ways of a society used to abundance. And politicians, with few exceptions, tend not to arouse prosperous businesspeople and comfortable consumers. To those who prod them they say, "I care about the environment," or "I am an environmentalist," as if all questions were answered by saying the word, and the public tends to let it go at that.

Much of the inertia that thwarts environmental concerns is a function of what we call "the economy." In our ordinary speech we liken it to an organism with a life of its own. We speak of it as strengthening, weakening, heating

165

up, cooling off, being slowed or stimulated, being healthy or depressed. We pay obsessive attention to this organism, and we zealously encourage its growth. Higher gross national product, higher profits, higher Dow Jones averages, more jobs, more housing starts, upturns in the "leading economic indicators"—these we equate with progress, health, and a better future, and nothing seems to make us realize that the growth we worship is fueled by finite resources and spews its dangerous wastes into a biosphere with finite powers of absorption. Few are teaching us that in the human economy, as in the economy of nature, growth within limits is health while growth without limits is disease. The symptoms of our irresponsibility are multiplying, but the growth economy remains virtually sacrosanct.

Even among environmentalists, the growth economy is a blind spot. Conditioned into the movement's reactive mode, we tend to find fault with outside entities—oil and timber corporations, polluting utilities or chemical plants, the Forest Service and other public agencies, agribusiness. Those entities have plenty to be faulted for. They need to be confronted and their irresponsible actions curtailed. But everyone who uses wood and paper products and consumes electrical energy and drives cars and eats the produce of corporate farms and blindly invests money for the highest return is accomplice to the excesses of the growth economy. As environmentalists we attempt to restrain it. To the extent that we consume in the habitual American way, we feed it. The organism is made of all of us.

It's true that environmentalism has successfully halted or curbed some depredations of the growth economy. But it's also true, and maybe in the long run more significant, that the fortunes of environmental organizations are substantially linked to the fortunes of the economy. When times are prosperous—at least for the middle and upper classes that traditionally form the environmental constituency—membership and contributions are high. When the economy enters a recession, as in 1990, membership and contributions fall off. Even among many of those sympathetic with its goals, environmentalism is seen not as a necessity but as a luxury, one of the first to be dispensed with when times are hard. Whether the environmental cause can succeed in this country with that basis of support —and with the movement's vitality, as measured in numbers of members and dollars, dependent on the vitality of the very growth economy that makes environmentalism necessary—is questionable at best.

The problem is that we as a people do not fundamentally believe that our excesses will do us harm. Native American cultures, by contrast, were constantly reminding themselves of that truth. A story from the Wasco people, collected by Jarold Ramsey in *Coyote Was Going There,* tells of a young man who is visited by a spirit Elk. The Elk empowers the boy as a great hunter, promising to provide for him in every necessity. In return, the boy must kill only what he needs, not more. But the boy is prodded by his human father into killing all the elk in the countryside, five

167

entire herds. He even tries, without knowing it, to kill his own spirit Elk. The Elk draws the boy deep into a lake, where he sees the spirits—in the story they are called persons—of all the animals he has slaughtered. The Elk rebukes him for breaking their pact and abandons him. The boy is cast out of the lake, goes home to explain his guilt to his gathered friends, and dies.

I have omitted much of the plot's complexity—in particular, the boy's divided allegiance between the spirit Elk and his human father, which gives his fall a tragic dimension—in order to distill what I understand to be the cautionary point: if you kill more animals than you need to live, you will die. Like Payatamu in the Zuni story, the boy breaks a reciprocal bond with nonhuman nature, and disaster results. And like the Zuni tale, the Wasco story was told through generations because it carried wisdom the tribe couldn't afford to forget.

Such wisdom doesn't arise from a vacuum. Indians were, and are, no more innately gifted with ecological awareness than we are. The people who walked into a New World twelve to thirty thousand years ago doubtless brought with them a heritage of customs and traditions, but they also may have come with something of the irresponsibility that European settlers later brought with them. The existence of stories like that of the boy and the Elk suggests that early Indians may have committed excesses amid the seemingly infinite abundance of North America and won their wisdom through hard experience. But the

Indians had a great expanse of time in which to learn responsibility, and were sufficiently limited in population and technology that they and their environment could recover from their mistakes. Our own situation is more precarious. If we can't find a way to teach ourselves and remember through time our own reciprocal bond with nature, we are capable of doing enormous damage to our world and ourselves.

But how can we learn the wisdom we need? If environmentalism remains a minority reactive force, if Leopold's land ethic has evolved as idea but not substantially as practice, if our economy stifles environmental values, if our own cultural heritage is inadequate to guide us, where will wisdom come from? I don't know. It may be that we will learn only through the experience of catastrophe. But possibly we may learn in a less bitter, dangerous, and stupid way. It will not happen by means of reactive environmentalism alone, important as that is. It will require something more than popular awareness of the ideas of ecology. I believe that to realize the ethical relationship to land that Leopold envisioned and Indians have lived, we need to rediscover— and perhaps are rediscovering—a religious relationship to the natural world.

Black Elk Speaks, the story of an Oglala Sioux warrior and seer, begins like this:

It is the story of all life that is holy and is good to tell, and of us two-leggeds sharing in it with the four-leggeds and the wings of the air and all green things; for these are children of one mother and their father is one Spirit.

Like Leopold, Black Elk sees land as a community to which humans belong. But he sees a particular kind of community —one of relationship by birth, a family. And it is a sacred family, whose mother is Earth and whose father is Spirit.

In Black Elk's words, as in the stories of Payatamu and the boy and the Elk, ecologically responsible behavior is implicit. You cherish all natural beings as you cherish your human family, for all are sisters and brothers, and all are manifestations of divinity. You are no more likely to injure the Earth than you are to injure your mother. If the Sun is the Father who sustains you, you will take pains to keep him rising. Every act required to maintain human life is of religious significance, undertaken with humility and reverence; every act embodies a complex understanding of humanity and nature evolved through thousands of years in the land of this continent where the rest of us are green newcomers. Taught in story, song, and ritual through generations, reciprocal responsibility with nature is assumed and thoroughly practiced.

To say this is not to idealize traditional Indian cultures. Those societies had severe limitations. Their people were acquainted with hardship and evil. But they had— and, insofar as traditional cultures survive, still have—an ecological awareness far superior to our own. In this regard, their traditions have much to teach us, and our situation is sufficiently grave that we should care very much about learning it. We are not likely to solve our ecological problems until responsible behavior becomes as immediate and deeply rooted in our culture as it was among the Indians. And that will only happen, I believe, when we regain a religious sense of nature akin to theirs.

The point is not that we should learn the Sioux language and perform the Sun Dance, or that we should plant corn in dry places and sing it up with Zuni songs and rituals. We can't simply borrow another culture's religious sensibility, evolved through ages, as we borrow a coat. Nor is it crucial to believe that certain words and actions cause the sun to come up. But it is very crucial to understand the sensibility from which such words and actions flow, to understand that the continuance of life depends on the thoughts, words, and acts of each of us, just as the rising of the Sun depended on Payatamu's daily pilgrimage, just as the boy's power depended on his honoring the pact he made with the spirit Elk.

An understanding of land as sacred and familial is obviously foreign to our secular worldview, and it may seem foreign to the Judeo-Christian tradition that forms the mainstream of what religious life we have. But as Wendell Berry has argued eloquently for years, Christians who hold the creation in contempt are not following Scripture but

171

defying it. One can't serve God by misusing or destroying His work. What's more, the Christian mystical tradition, ranging back through Julian of Norwich, Hildegard of Bingen, and Saint Francis of Assisi, affirms the oneness and sacredness of nature in a way that Black Elk would have understood. Our European ancestors for many centuries felt themselves to be part of a cosmic chain encompassing all Being. And far deeper in the past, before the Christian era, our forebears were tribespeople who saw a holiness around them to which they felt themselves somehow akin. The sense of the sacred family is not something new and unattained, like Leopold's land ethic. It is both a cultural relict and a latent possibility in us all.

More than a possibility. In a diverse variety of forms, the sense of the sacred family is very much alive today in this country and the rest of the industrialized world. It is present in the life and work of Wendell Berry, and in others who find in Christian tradition both the justification and the necessity of responsible ecological behavior. It is present in the concept of Gaia, the living organism of Earth, developed as a scientific hypothesis by James Lovelock and embraced as a religious as well as scientific idea by thousands of his readers. It is present in the revival of interest in ancient pagan rituals and healing practices associated with the Goddess. It is present in the work of Gary Snyder, and in others who express in the terms of Eastern religions their sense of divine immanence and the kinship of all being. It is present in the American nature religion of Emerson, Thoreau, Whitman, and Muir, mutated and reexpressed in the twentieth century by such poets and writers as Robinson Jeffers, A. R. Ammons, and Annie Dillard. It is present in the broad biocentric view through time of the deep ecologists. It is present in the spiritual dimension of the Green and ecofeminist movements. And it is present in thousands, perhaps millions, of individuals such as myself whose experiences of the natural world have a religious character that calls for expression but seems to fit no established form.

I don't suggest that these various religious manifestations can be reduced to the same belief, but they have much in common with each other and with American Indian religions: a sense of the sacredness of nature, a view of humanity as one life form related to all others, and a recognition of our need to assume responsibility toward the nonhuman world. Taken together, these modern versions of the sacred family may constitute an emerging spiritual rediscovery of ourselves and nature. And such a rekindling of our religious imagination, it seems to me, is as important to our future as any amount of letter writing, lobbying, demonstrating, or direct action, because it represents a potential change of the magnitude I believe we need. It represents a force, very likely the only force, that stands a chance of overcoming our prevailing secular religion—our orthodox and primitive belief in the growth economy and the unlimited development of technology.

When those givens are called into question, the cry immediately goes up—even from many who are sympathetic toward environmental causes—that we can't go *back* to the life of an earlier time, that anyone who suggests such a thing is a simplistic Luddite. It is true that we cannot wholly abandon our present way of life, and we do not need to. But in this century we have reached the point where the dangers of continued economic growth and technological development have begun to outweigh the benefits. To acknowledge this is only realistic. And isn't it simplistic to assume that the cure for the troubles caused by growth and development will be found in more growth and more development? Sometimes, as anyone who has lost a trail in the forest knows, going back to find your way again is the most practical thing to do. Sometimes it is the only thing to do.

And paradoxically, to limit voluntarily our economic growth and technological power, to relinquish some of our control over nature in order to join it again, would not weaken us. It would empower us. In withdrawing from the sacred family, we have not only shed its responsibilities, we have also lost its privileges. The cost is the loneliness of our disconnected state, the great bereavement of no longer knowing ourselves at home in the natural matrix that gave us birth. True power comes from relatedness. Where is the power among us, in all our expertise and technological might, to equal that of Payatamu, who participates in the mysteriously benevolent power of the sunrise? What we can only watch from the bare room of our rationality and greet with a diffuse aesthetic response, Payatamu is part of.

In the Zuni story, the world lies dark after Payatamu is beheaded by the witch. Until his body can be found and restored and his ritual practice renewed, the Sun Father won't rise. Payatamu's brothers know they won't be able to find him by themselves, and so, in humility, they ask the help of their grandfathers who live in all the directions— mountain lion, bear, badger, eagle, vulture, true coyote, juniper coyote, and crow. Each searches and fails, and then the brothers ask their "father who lives at the nadir, the mole"—the slightest of animals, and, of course, the one best suited to tracking in darkness. The mole finds Payatamu's severed head in the witch's jar and teams with the hawk and the owl to steal it. Payatamu is restored, and the story goes: "aaaaaaAAAAAA THE SUN CAME UP."

In such a world, humans are not alone. Their relations are all around them, each with special powers and each empowering the others. It takes the entire family together, the great and the small, the human and the animal, to keep the world unfolding as it should. The mole says, "If he's alone it won't work," and his comment is true for every being alive.

Our own world, the signs are clear, is working less and less well. It will take many wills laboring together to turn it back toward health. Remembering the sacred family, I believe, has an important part to play in that change.

It cannot be made to happen, by proselytizing or persuasion, and it will not happen overnight—religious transformation, like ecological disaster, creeps slowly. We are not used to seeing nature as holy and akin to ourselves. But we are capable of seeing it so, and that way lies the best hope we have of avoiding the calamities now looming and those we don't yet discern. The path of the sacred family leads back, then forward, toward a world in which the very term "environment" may become unnecessary, a world in which we do not act upon the land but in and of the land, so at home in our surroundings that it makes no sense to speak of an external environment. We *are* what we act upon and what acts upon us. When we separate ourselves, we come to no good. If we're alone, says the mole, it won't work.

The Poem of Being

I look for the way
things will turn
out spiralling from a center,
the shape
things will take to come forth in

so that the birch tree white
touched black at branches
will stand out
wind-glittering
totally its apparent self:

I look for the forms
things want to come as

from what black wells of possibility,
how a thing will
unfold . . .

   —A. R. Ammons

177

THE THEORY OF evolution, as I understand it, holds that no mind or force intended humans to be. We exist, but we did not have to exist. Nature happened upon us, as it has happened upon millions of other species, living and long extinct. Life is not a set of completed artifacts but a dynamic, ongoing process, aimed at no particular end and proceeding by no plan. Among human activities, the aimless creativity of evolution resembles the play of children at their most spontaneous and imaginative, or the kind of walking or travel that holds to no one direction or destination. But even more closely, it seems to me, evolution resembles the creative activity of the poet.

In my writing, the making of something new proceeds by a slow, unsure development. There is no outline, no blueprint, just a nearsighted wanting-to-create that accrues a sense of what it is making only as it enters and engages the work. Like the way of evolution, the way of the poet is a way of experimentation, of trying things out, of proceeding haltingly through existing forms into new ones. Nature makes life-things, the poet makes word-things, and it seems to me there is something akin in the creative intelligence of each.

The species that evolution bodies forth are characterized by wholeness, soundness of form, and peculiar beauty. They are so well suited to their surroundings, so adept at what they do to sustain their lives, that many humans have assumed a divine plan in nature, an intentionality on the part of a conscious, all-powerful, and all-knowing God. How could anything as remarkable as a monarch butterfly, it seems reasonable to ask, with its complex form, singular beauty, and precise long-distance navigational system, have merely *happened* by means of blind and accidental processes?

It could have happened in much the same way a poem happens. Those attributes of living things—wholeness, soundness, peculiar beauty—are attributes also of the best poems, the best pieces of any art. As with plants and animals, a well-realized poem conveys a sense of necessity and even inevitability; it gives the impression of being the way it is because it had to be. But it didn't have to be. Poets know that much of the beauty and wholeness of their work not only can arise unintentionally, by lack of direction, but can *only* arise in that way. The right elements and relation of elements evolve through what Rainer Maria Rilke called a "wise blindness"—a process that takes months or years, generates many mistakes along the way, and cannot be forced by conscious prompting. The finished poem, necessary and inevitable as it might seem, is composed of many unforeseen emergences growing out of an engagement with language. Just as reasonably, a monarch butterfly can be viewed as the result of unforeseen emergences growing out of the engagement of life with the planet Earth. As I look at a butterfly or a great poem, the question that occurs to me is not how such a thing could have happened accidentally—I ask how anything that unlikely and beautiful could have been planned.

A poet, of course, is a conscious being, and poems are not simply received from the unconscious. As a work assumes its rough wholeness, the modeling of deliberate choice becomes increasingly important to its development. And some of the greatest poems, particularly longer narrative works such as the *Divine Comedy*, surely are guided from their inception by an overall plan. The butterfly and the poem do not arise in exactly the same way.

Yet I can't help thinking they arise in something *close* to the same way. Nature at large, though it shows no sign of consciousness or intentionality, unquestionably does possess a tendency to elaborate itself into forms and relationships of intricate complexity, and the means of that tendency—natural selection—might be called unconscious choice. Without knowing that it chooses, nature chooses nonetheless from the possibilities raised by genetic variation, according to the standard of fittedness to the environment—over time, those forms best fitted perpetuate themselves, those less well fitted do not. And if scientist James Lovelock's Gaia hypothesis is right, the living skin of Earth is continually making unconscious choices as a single organism, regulating climate and the composition of oceans and atmosphere in order to maintain the best conditions for life. Is that unaware choosing so far removed from the process of the conscious poet, who chooses according to a different standard—a notion of aesthetic wholeness—from among the possibilities raised by the unconscious mind? The poet's awareness is secondary, picking among the words, images, and connections generated by the deep intelligence of the imagination, as nature picks among the life forms raised by its own unconscious intelligence.

Some of nature's choosing, of course, occurs without regard to fittedness, perpetuation of life, or any other standard. Random catastrophic events have apparently had huge influence on the course of evolution. It is becoming increasingly certain, for instance, that the dinosaurs died off not because they were ponderous and slow-witted, but because of a sun-dimming dust cloud raised sixty-five million years ago either by the impact of a massive asteroid or by large-scale volcanic eruptions. And much earlier in Earth's history, a still greater cataclysm of unknown nature—the Permian extinction—may have destroyed 95 percent of all species then inhabiting the planet. Those disasters, though, were not just terminations. They were also beginnings. With each mass extinction—there have been about half a dozen, altogether—came a quick proliferation of new species, new forms emerging out of old ones, new possibilities rising into being. One of those possibilities, whose way was prepared when the dinosaurs disappeared and the adaptive rodent-like mammals of the time prospered, was us. The asteroid or volcanoes that killed over half the life on Earth gave our remote ancestors their chance.

It may be disquieting to consider that human existence owes itself not only to the unconscious choosing of evolution, but also to brute volcanic force or the random mechanics of interplanetary space. But there is justice, and even necessity, in that kind of chance intervention. The works of the poet or painter, as they evolve, are sometimes startled by what poet W. S. Di Piero calls "the cranky shriek of accident"—chance intrusion, from within the artist's psyche or from without—which cracks open an unfinished piece and permits it to evolve further. The artist learns to be receptive to that kind of accident, whose effect is not to reduce the work to chaos but to allow its progress toward, in Di Piero's words, "an unforeseeable order worked into place by the aggressions of chance." His phrase could apply as aptly to the artistry of nature. Why shouldn't evolution, the poem of earthly life, itself take shape through the aggressions of chance as it shifts and streams through its own unforeseeable orders?

The kinship I sense between the human imagination and the imagination of nature is hardly an equal relationship. No poet or scientist or any human being can make a monarch butterfly, let alone the ecosystem of a rainforest. The intricate profusion of life on this planet is engendered by a creative intelligence so profoundly abler, wilder, and more original than my own that I can only feel awe before it. Religion is the tying of human life to mysteries greater than itself, and I can conceive of no greater or more beau-

tiful mystery than the mystery claimed by science as fact—
that we are bodily imaginations of three and a half billion
years of a generative energy that never intended us but
brought us to life, and moves through us, and everything
else that lives, toward further imaginings that neither it nor
we can know. It is that dynamic intelligence, finding its
way amid the vagaries of chance not by plan but by doing,
that I hold divine.

Historically, of course, evolution and religion have
mixed like oil and water. Charles Darwin chose not to
publish his theory for twenty years because he knew it
would set off a storm, particularly among the Christian
orthodox. If humanity has evolved from other life forms,
then we are not a special creation in God's image but only
another animal among many. And if life is developing aim-
lessly, changing through time toward no particular goal,
how can it reflect the effort and concern of an omniscient,
all-powerful deity? One worldview threatens another: science against religion, materialism versus spirituality and
faith. As religion attacks the perceived threat from science,
science jealously guards its private property against the least
taint of religion.

But there was no such pronounced antagonism in the
minds of those who first conceived the idea of evolution.
Darwin's grandfather, whose writings probably sparked the
notion in Darwin's own psyche, speculated that all warm-
blooded animals arose from one primary strand of life,

and he extolled the idea as a sign of the infinite power of God. (I don't know how he accounted for cold-blooded animals.) And Darwin himself seems to have recognized no essential conflict between religion and science in his monumental discovery. He compared the continuous branching of species to the biblical Tree of Life, and at the end of *The Origin of Species* he writes of God and nature in the same awed tone:

> There is grandeur in this view of life, with its several powers, having been originally breathed by the Creator into a few forms or into one; and that, whilst this planet has gone cycling on according to the fixed law of gravity, from so simple a beginning endless forms most beautiful and most wonderful have been, and are being evolved.

And Darwin, though his name has become practically synonymous with evolution, isn't the only authority on the subject. His mind achieved a clear formulation that revolutionized the biological sciences and is still revolutionizing our human view of ourselves, but the notion of evolving life was very much in the air during the nineteenth century, and not only in the circles of science. Walt Whitman, writing in America while *The Origin of Species* was still a manuscript in Darwin's desk drawer, discovered himself to be deeply related to other orders of nature:

The Poem of Being

> *I find I incorporate gneiss, coal, long-threaded moss, fruits,*
> *   grains, esculent roots,*
> *And am stucco'd with quadrupeds and birds all over . . .*

The writing of "Song of Myself" opened to Whitman's inner gaze the same long vistas of evolutionary time that so moved Darwin with their grandeur:

> *Rise after rise bow the phantoms before me,*
> *Afar down I see the huge first Nothing, I know I was even*
> *   there,*
> *I waited unseen and always, and slept through the lethargic*
> *   mist,*
> *And took my time, and took no hurt from the fetid carbon.*
> *. . . . .*
> *Before I was born out of my mother generations guided me,*
> *My embryo has never been torpid, nothing could overlay it.*
>
> *For it the nebula cohered to an orb,*
> *The long slow strata piled to rest it on,*
> *Vast vegetables gave it sustenance,*
> *Monstrous sauroids transported it in their mouths and*
> *   deposited it with care.*

Whitman's evolution is not the same as Darwin's. He unscientifically assumes a direction in the process, an inevitability that led from the first Nothing to his human existence, as if he were the point of evolution's progression. But when Whitman uses the personal pronoun, his personal being is only part of what he means. The Self he sings is composed of an expanding series of concentric rings: Walt Whitman, part of humankind, part of all life, part of the Earth, part of the Cosmos itself. He perceives those rings as one and the same even as they are several and different, and when he says "I" in "Song of Myself" he means them all— "I am large, I contain multitudes." His evolution is not a scientific hypothesis but an intuited religion, a pantheistic vision in which all forms of life are not only interesting, not only grand and beautiful, but divine. Darwin holds to the traditional Christian dichotomy between God and nature, Creator and created, but Whitman sees them as one. "I hear and behold God in every object," he writes, "yet understand God not in the least."

I have never doubted the existence of God, but not until I read Whitman, and Robinson Jeffers, did I hear my sense of God expressed. Why, I have always wondered, would God be some dissociated spirit? Why would God be anything other than nature and the evolving universe itself? How could it be that one life form on one planet in one solar system in one galaxy in one cluster of galaxies on one fringe of the cosmos is made in God's image, and only one? How much more plausible it seems that all forms of life, and all forms of matter that gave birth to life, are images of God because they *are* God, God's very body and spirit in one, realizing itself in time. Evolution and divinity need not be antagonistic concepts but different names for the same thing, the Being that is always a Becoming. Whitman calls it the "perpetual journey":

> *Urge and urge and urge,*
> *Always the procreant urge of the world.*
>
> *Out of the dimness opposite equals advance, always substance*
>   *and increase, always sex,*
> *Always a knit of identity, always distinction, always a breed*
>   *of life.*

As well as sex and increase, of course, the journey is made of violence and death. Nature's genius, like our own, is not wholly benign and pleasant. It has conjured a world in which animals devour one another, in which populations live or die according to the chances of food chain and weather. Asteroids wipe out thousands of species, exploding supernovae in distant space perhaps vaporize entire worlds of evolved beings. The sun that gives us life, like all suns, will burn out. The universe develops with no special regard for human beings or for any particular form of life, and thus its workings can seem brute and terrifying.

But as Robinson Jeffers tried for half a century to convey, nature seems brutish only because we, in our self-consciousness, value our individual lives and our species far more highly than nature values us. We see ourselves and the external world through a screen of moral, political, and aesthetic concepts, and while those concepts may serve vital purposes in our dealings among ourselves, they do not describe the universe outside the small arena of our tribal affairs. To the extent that we are able, in Jeffers's words, "to uncenter the human mind from itself," to see more as conscious nature and less as particular human beings, that which seems repellent and terrifying in nature is transformed. Watching frenzied seabirds attack schools of fish off the California coast, Jeffers sees clearly the brutality of the scene, but also something beyond brutality:

> *What*
> *hysterical greed!*
> *What a filling of pouches! the mob*
> *Hysteria is nearly human—these decent birds!—as if they*
> *were finding*
> *Gold in the street. It is better than gold,*
> *It can be eaten: and which one in all this fury of wildfowl*
> *pities the fish?*
> *No one certainly. Justice and mercy*
> *Are human dreams, they do not concern the birds nor the fish*
> *nor eternal God.*
> *However—look again before you go.*
> *The wings and the wild hungers, the wave-worn skerries, the*
> *bright quick minnows*

Living in terror to die in torment—
Man's fate and theirs—and the island rocks and immense
ocean beyond, and Lobos
Darkening above the bay: they are beautiful?
That is their quality: not mercy, not mind, not goodness, but
the beauty of God.

The beauty Jeffers celebrates is much broader than ordinary notions of natural beauty. It is not prettiness or sublimity, not grace of form necessarily; it comprehends those aspects of nature that we find attractive and those that appall and horrify us. It is the essential integrity of things as nature has made them, their innate propriety of form and relation. "Integrity is wholeness," Jeffers writes,

the greatest beauty is
Organic wholeness, the wholeness of life and things, the divine
beauty of the universe. Love that, not man
Apart from that . . .

Beauty of wholeness is the condition toward which nature's imagination tends—a dynamic wholeness, never finished, never completely achieved. Fish become gulls and pelicans, sea cliffs erode and rise somewhere else, continents drift on currents of magma, the stars themselves run the course of their fiery lives and spew their substance into space, where eventually their atoms come to compose the furnaces of other stars, the substances of other worlds. We and our planet embody the lives and deaths of innumerable suns over billions of years of cosmic time. We have materialized in the long becoming of the universe and will lend our matter to its ongoing, to its forms and orders that range far past what we can know.

To us, as to fish and sea birds, the universe that is God offers no immortality of the soul, no fable of personal salvation devised to ease the fear of dying. It offers, simply and miraculously, itself—its new and ancient beauty composed of all that is. And to humans, more than to fish and birds, it offers also the capacity to perceive that beauty and hold it in mind. That we or anything exist at all is the first gift, the source of all religion—in Whitman's words, "the puzzle of puzzles, / And that we call Being." The second gift, as unforeseen and incalculable, is consciousness. In us, and to various degrees in other animals, and almost certainly in other beings on other worlds, the unconscious unfolding of the universe has surfaced into knowledge of itself. In this small way on Earth, like a child awakening into self-awareness, the universe begins to see where it has come from and where it may tend, and it sees the beauty of its journey.

Something like that beauty, I believe, is what the poet tries to realize in the work of words. Like nature's, the poet's imagination tends toward organic wholeness, toward the unforeseeable fruition of the inchoate impulse that wanted life as a poem. I see through my own mental screen, I realize, and it is possible that I merely project my personal sense of creativity upon the workings of nature, that there is no actual kinship between the two. I can only answer that it seems more likely that nature projects itself in me—that the experience of my own imaginative life opens my awareness to the similar but primary creativity that gave me birth, the imagination that works in the language of things, unspeakably vaster, freer, and more original than my own. Since time was born some thirteen billion years ago, that first imagination has arrayed itself in an expanding and ever-elaborating cosmos of forms, and for me the joy of writing poems comes from taking part in some small way in that same kind of creative emergence, from realizing as best I can in my psyche's own cosmos the unconscious desire in the heart of the infinite that has given birth to monarch butterflies, to spiral galaxies, to the endless poem of being.

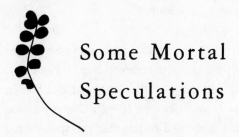

Some Mortal
Speculations

AS I STEPPED into the shed yesterday morning looking for a rake, a silent commotion caught my eye. A blue fly was floundering in a web by the door—wings blurring, its abdomen curling almost to its head as it strained to pull loose, rocking and bouncing and tearing the web. And the spider was just above, dancing with all its legs, dancing down and nimbly retreating. Half the fly's size, a dull red color, it descended and climbed, never still. Once as it came down it might have managed to jab in its venom; in any case the fly weakened, arching feebly as the spider wrapped its legs and started to carry it away. The damaged web tore under the spider's weight, and tore again. The spider left its bundle and laid new strands, but they too gave way, and for a moment it was still. Slowly then, ceremoniously I thought, it placed its legs around the fly's head and clasped it to its belly. For a moment the spider moved slightly, as if adjusting a ritual posture, then spider and fly were still.

When I returned half an hour later, and at intervals

193

throughout the afternoon, the spider hadn't moved but both had changed. The fly seemed shrunken, the spider swollen. The fly's blue gloss had gone dull; the spider's abdomen shone. And I might have imagined it—the light was too poor to be sure—but it seemed to me that the spider's red belly now had a blue tinge. This morning when I looked there was only the fly's dry husk, a dot of white web attached to one eye.

As I watched that encounter, I felt wildly different things: pity at the fly's helplessness, respect for the spider's mastery, the horror of a life sucked out of its shell. But if such an event is horrible, it is the most commonplace horror in the world. It occurs billions of times every second, *this* second, countless lives slipping into the lives of others— field mouse swelling the king snake, krill becoming body of blue whale, deer disappearing into coyote and magpie and the blooming generations of microbes that carry dead life into darkness and return it to the light. Horrible? Cruel? No more so than the compost, that black distillation of death that I spade into the garden. If it is cruel that a red spider should sustain itself, and thus survive to make more red spiders, and so spin its evolutionary line a little deeper into the openness of time, then cruelty must be part of the very genius that brought spiders and flies and other creatures into being, and which continues to elaborate life into unlikely and beautiful forms.

And yet—some weeks ago, on the brick walkway

along the end of the house, I almost stepped on a small beetle. I stooped to get a better look at its odd jerky movements and saw that it was trying, without much success, to shake off a mob of black ants that were darting all around and over it. When the beetle managed to free one leg, a new ant would immediately clamp on and hang, a dragging weight. Sometimes two or three at once gripped a leg; others raced over the beetle's body, trying its armor, as the awkward creature flicked and shook and attempted to walk.

I watched for as long as I could, and even those few seconds were almost unbearable—though I don't know why. I have a fairly strong stomach for the depredations of animals. The cat torments a gopher for half an hour before killing it, or sits with a lizard's twitching tail hanging out of its mouth, and I don't mind watching. I understand the cat to be sharpening its nerves through such playful delay, much as it sharpens its claws on the porch post, and I admire its keen intelligence. But weren't the ants that swarmed the beetle displaying their own intelligence? Weren't they acting out their own instinctive genius, not too distant from the genius I admire in the cat? In fact, as they worked together to bring down their enormous prey, didn't they mirror my own ancestors of fifty thousand years ago, those little dodging men who harried and pricked the groaning mastodon until it fell?

I rescued the beetle, or tried to. I took a pine needle and poked off the ants, rubbed them out, and turned the beetle loose some twenty feet away. Almost immediately, other ants clamped on to its legs. I carried it around the corner of the house and set it down again, and within seconds it was attacked by three ants. That beetle was rife with distress, and any ant could smell it. Finally, I dropped it in the dry grass of the field. It walked away, spry-seeming, but as I watched it I didn't have much confidence either in its longevity or in my reflexive gesture that had temporarily kept it alive.

It seems likely that humankind is the only animal capable of the altruism to rescue a member of a different species from death. But I wouldn't have saved that beetle from a towhee. If I had stepped on it accidentally I would have felt a twinge of remorse, but nothing more. Clearly my concern rose less from pure altruism than from a horror of ants, or some still deeper source. And so I find myself squarely in the middle of a contradiction, unable or unwilling to be reconciled with a fundamental truth of nature: that a beetle's death by ants is as proper and seemly as a death by towhee or a death by old age. In the natural economy, any death is proper that nourishes other life, which means that any death is proper. A beetle, a fly, a million dinosaurs—where they fell other life rose, if only in waves of microbes and a new exuberance of flora.

We humans, as always, want to exempt ourselves. In life we increasingly encapsulate our bodies from the organic processes of nature, as if we had no connection with them, and in death we attempt the same, armoring our remains in crypts and coffins and steel ash boxes. Like altruism, our respectful treatment of our dead has been cited as a quality that defines us as human, something more than the animals. But what it chiefly defines, it seems to me, is simply our discontent with mortality. We don't like to die; and if we have to die, we don't like to think of our own dead bodies feeding other creatures.

In evolution's long streaming through time, individual lives don't count for much. Nature thinks in populations, in species, in systems and relationships. It thinks in process and continuation. Individuals are bubbles in the current, briefly here and gone, important only as expressions of what has come before and as constituents of what will follow. That plight presents no emotional problems for pine trees or sparrows, but it does for us because we are aware that we are bubbles. What actually best defines us, and accounts for our other defining characteristics, is our acute consciousness.

The beetle obviously was aware of its plague of ants, and wanted them off. No doubt it felt the stings of their jaws, and possibly even the scurry of their feet across its back. Maybe it even felt an indistinct kind of rage or fear, but almost certainly it felt no horror at its impending death. It was I, watching, who felt the horror—and not so much for the beetle's sake, I now realize, as for my own. The swarming ants repulsed me because I saw a sign of my own fate there. Someday my body will feed other life, and it won't be a towhee that it feeds.

Ever since I've been aware of death I've been intensely afraid of it. As a child, lying awake in bed, I used to imagine it as an endless drifting among icy stars—and my terror came not from that cold vision but from knowing that even the vision was a lie, that death meant seeing nothing, feeling nothing, no consciousness ever again, no *me*. There was no consolation, only the eventual distraction of other thoughts, and sleep.

As Darwin saw, there is grandeur in the prospect of evolutionary time. To be part of this unlikely process, this varied ongoing river that rises out of mystery and tends into further mystery, is a kind of consolation. But it's an abstract consolation. I can't see the fullness of evolutionary time, and except in rare ecstatic moments, I don't feel part of it. Its grandeur is an idea, its beauty as coolly remote as the stars. And both its grandeur and its beauty dissolve all too easily in my fearful mind and leave me thinking of a grotesque parade, a slow blind wave that raises bits of life to sentience and then buries them forever—individuals, families, entire species wandering their weather of chances and then going under as the blind wave rolls on, indifferent, meaningless as clouds of dust in the absolute zero of infinite space.

But that too, of course, is abstraction. What I know for sure is nothing as large as that, whether beautiful or terrifying or both, and nothing as remote. My mind, like my hands, is best suited to the grasping of smaller things, things that happen close in front of me, things I can see and turn slowly in memory and see again, in imagination's second light. It is only a tenuous bubble that I inhabit, but how bright and various the world looks from within it. How vividly I see the beetle I could hardly bear to watch before, how it flicks and lurches, how quickly the tiny black ants dart over its shell, how clearly I recall the shiny spider, the dull shrunken fly—they and a thousand other things that my eyes have gathered are lit by my need to see them, to see into the mystery to which each is a clue, the mystery whose answer somehow is death.

I remember my first winter in eastern Oregon, awaking one night to an intensely strange and moving sound, a frenzied chorus of falsetto yips and howls—the cold starlit dark on fire with coyote cries. I lay warm in bed, my entire body tingling. It was a killing song, of course. A deer or sheep lay bleeding on the snow, never to rise, but what ecstatic music the coyotes made of that life they had claimed. In an alchemy that lasted only seconds, it seemed to me that the blood of the dead and the ancient strain of the coyotes' own blood rose together, transformed wholly into song. I can't say what that singing meant to the coyotes. Its intensity, its quality of utter emptying into sound, made me think that it meant more to them than mere food. But whatever they felt in their singing, for me it was not horror but fierce beauty. It was joy that rose in me, like some forgotten song of my own.

Death must have been both clearer and more mysterious—and perhaps easier to face—when I was one of those dodging men who swarmed with spears around the mastodon. When we killed our meat or else starved, and sometimes died in the killing, when things flared with spirit and every movement of the world was magic, there must have been moments when our own throats burned with involuntary cries, when our own blood surged up and sounded itself in the quiet of the land. In those moments we sang triumph, fear, awe—all the feelings we had no words for, or not words enough. And perhaps more than the coyotes we sang our loneliness, our sense of isolation in a world from which we had already begun to separate ourselves, our smallness and transience in the depths of night.

Whether or not it was my own distant past that moved me in those coyote cries, I know in any case that they were beautiful. I suppose that beauty, like cruelty, is a category of the human mind, a projection that we cast about with our consciousness. Yet beauty seems so abundant in nature, things seem so thoroughly and extravagantly filled with it, that I have to think it *is* in things, their fundamental fact—and that I've learned to appreciate it in coyotes but not completely yet in ants and spiders. They too are beautiful, and the deaths of other lives compose their beauty, as the deaths of other lives compose our own. All of us are in motion, rising out of previous forms and advancing into new ones, and beauty is the best name I know for the ways in which our shape-shifting nature pursues its changes.

And that is abstraction again, an attempt to say more than I know. What I know, finally, and can't shake loose from, is that the bubble breaks for all of us. For me. The beauty of things will go on, but I will not be alive to witness it. When other lives rise on what I was, the familiar light of my awareness will not rise with them. I who hold the world in mind will then be held in the world, without a mind, lost in what I once looked upon. And so at forty I look carefully at things that live, because everything I see is hieroglyphic of what I might become. Scrub jay scratching in the underbrush, gray squirrel leaping the gap of limbs, the exact aimlessness of blowing leaves—I will be there, and deep in the burrowings of roots and worms, in the ants' long marches and the lizard's crouch, in the spider's stillness and its nimble dance.

I look, and nature answers, speaking in a thousand things. It is alive to my longing, it repays my vanishing in advance. This evening, just before sundown, I heard a whistling out in the field. After a few minutes walking and looking I found the source: two great horned owls, an adult and a young, facing away on the outreaching limb of a solitary oak. They were moving, rocking forward and turning toward each other, and I thought perhaps they were preening. Then suddenly—maybe because the mother heard my approach—they turn on the limb and face me, and I see what they are doing.

The mother tilts forward and rips off a piece of some kind of prey that she holds against the limb with her talons. As she straightens with food in her bill, the fledgling, whistling hoarsely, grabs it with his bill and bolts it down. And so they continue their meal, the mother tearing the small animal without pause or hurry, the fledgling whistling and eating, as the last slant sun turns their mottled brown and white to reddish gold. When they have finished, the mother flies from the limb and the young one follows, the two of them drifting on motionless wings, low and silent over the dry grasses and down the hill, disappearing in the darkening trees.

The Trail Home

THIS AFTERNOON, as I scanned the oaks
in the field for the red-shouldered hawk that yelps like a
puppy, I turned my binoculars across the draw, toward
Country Way. I saw that the newest house over there is
nearly finished, on the outside at least—a massive pink villa
with a red-tile roof, resplendent in the sun. A man was
puttering around the place, planting shrubs and flowers in
raw slopes of dirt, piling construction scraps. For long intervals he would stand still, looking around, then he'd move
on to plant something else. He and his work looked very
small in front of his enormous home.

Big new houses are one of the life forms local to this
area, and unlike foxes and wren-tits they are easy to observe.
In the manner of other species, they adapt in different ways
to their environment. Some are built low, in gray or natural
wood tones, blending with oaks down in folds of the hill-
sides so as barely to be seen. Others—especially the very
newest ones, like the pink villa—stand out boldly, often at
the very crown of a hill, proclaiming themselves like birds

in breeding plumage. Many seem to appear almost instantly, as if plopped down overnight, while some are many months in the building, even a year or two. I watched one of them evolve to a framework skeleton and suddenly stop, its bright studs dulling toward the color of the bleached summer grass. A Tudor place on our own side of the draw, just over the field's brink from our cottage, has remained roofless for more than a year now, bundles of shakes and rolls of tarpaper waiting on its rafters.

We don't know any of the people who live across the draw, though I did meet one at a distance once. As I scanned my binoculars over there I spotted a man in shorts scanning *me,* or my direction anyway. We didn't wave, and I quickly lowered the glasses. Whatever we know of those distant neighbors we know from the size and styles of their homes, and from what the UPS delivery man tells us. He has peeked inside of new, half-million-dollar mansions in which a couple, or a single man, lived in a single furnished room, the rest bare and waiting. Such owners are trying to buy time until their finances steady; for some it never happens, and the next addition to their empty house is a FOR SALE sign.

It seems an odd way of life, building those huge structures, moving in, moving on. In matters of money and taste, and probably a host of other things, those villa-people are very different from us, very alien. But maybe not in every respect. This cottage at the end of a trail, which my

wife and I rent, is my twenty-ninth dwelling in forty years
—I recalled them the other day while driving I-280 to San
Francisco. This is our third summer here. How many more,
we can't say—very likely only one or two. Our cottage
would probably fit easily in the living room of that new
pink villa, yet I felt a certain kinship with the man I
watched this afternoon. As he knelt with trowel and shrubs,
as he stood quietly gazing, it seemed to me he was trying
to make connection with his new home, trying to locate
himself as he located his plants. He was testing the ground
with roots.

The little framed vegetable plot I tend on our own
hillside is the same kind of attempt. It's gaining the force
of ritual with me, to put in a garden anyplace I expect to
stay long enough to taste what I plant. I want produce with
better flavor than Safeway's, of course, but if that were all,
I could buy it at the farm stands. My father, for most of his
life an itinerant labor organizer, grew a small patch of beans
and tomatoes wherever he lit. When I remember him I see
him in a loose white T-shirt with a hoe in his hands, a
Chesterfield in his mouth, and a certain serenity around
him that he found in no other realm of his life. I suspect
that some of the tomatoes' sweetness for him was what it is
for me—the taste of permanence in a life of continual movement.

I don't know what the man of the pink villa was
thinking this afternoon, but as I watched him standing

there, looking around, drifting on to another job of planting or cleaning up, I imagined that he was trying to learn
a language, the same language I want to learn. Or want to
remember. Many around the world speak it clearly, pre-
cisely, naturally—but the villa-man and I, and millions of
others in this country where the average family moves once
every four years, have a hard time with it. We skim freely
from place to place, home to home, reasonably happy and
very possessive of our independence, but also just a bit
baffled, a bit stifled in our easy movement, sure of what
belongs to us but not at all sure of what we belong to.
Fluent in mobility, we try haltingly to learn the alphabet
of place.

The way to learn it, I suppose, is just to do it—to
stop skimming and settle down, to make a commitment to
a place and stay there. I have older friends, people I respect
greatly, who have done just that, and their engagement
with their surroundings is one of the things I both admire
and envy about them. Wally and Mary, our friends and
landlords, have lived just up the hill for over forty years.
The Monterey pines they planted when they built their
house have grown to over seventy feet, and the native oaks
have crept up around the place and half-enclosed it in the
grove. There is an ease about Wally as he complains of the
heavy clay soil, when he remembers certain storms and
certain droughts, when he and Mary try to remember between them when they planted a certain shrub or tree. All

their seasons here have woven a loose, comfortable clothing around their lives. They know where they are in a way I probably never will.

It seems that some important aspect of every place I live is always wrong, or insufficient, or incomplete. My wife and I love this three-room cottage we inhabit, hidden away on the side of a hill where a grove of live oaks meets a half-wild field, where besides Wally and Mary our closest neighbors are raccoons and deer, where a hundred-yard walk along a trail separates us from our cars and the nearest road. But we need more than my little garden to support us, we have to drive that road, and our greater place—the amorphous suburbia of the mid–San Francisco Peninsula, with its traffic jams, smog, and fast pace of life—doesn't suit us nearly as well as our oaks and field. There are too many people, and too many of them are just like us—transient, unsettled, passing through. It's a hard place to feel at home. And even if we did, how could we possibly afford the $200,000 it would take to buy a house not much bigger than our cottage?

As often as not, of course, there are positive reasons for moving on. My father traveled constantly and uprooted his family several times because there was union organizing to be done, work that helped human lives, in different towns and cities. And I came to the Peninsula from a place I loved—a rented house on a ranch in eastern Oregon—because of a very lucky opportunity, a graduate writing fellowship at Stanford. I stayed because the fellowship turned into a teaching job. But the job has a three-year limit; after that it's catch-as-catch-can, a course here and maybe a course there, and I'll be looking. When an opportunity arises, for me or for my engineer wife, we'll move on and break the ground for a tomato patch somewhere else.

The Plains Indians led a nomadic life too. But theirs was a patterned mobility, a response to seasonal shiftings and the availability of various foods, a cyclical wandering that kept bringing them back to known, loved, and revered places. I would feel differently if my movements constellated in such a meaningful way, or if I were part of an epic migration like that of the gray whales we watch off Point Reyes, the whales that spend the greater part of their lives swimming six thousand miles between the Bering Sea and the warm lagoons of Baja California. But my wanderings are separate and random: I am one erratic atom in a field of such atoms, all excited in our various ways by discontent, opportunity, and that sheer restlessness that seems deeply ingrained in the American character. And most of my friends are no different. I have learned to keep my address book in pencil, and there are parts of pages worn practically through with repeated erasures.

As I grow older, though, two slow changes give me hope that I might eventually arrive at some sense of place. I am staying longer in the places I live, several years instead of several months. And partly as a consequence of that, I am learning to pay attention to where I happen to be. I moved to the eastern Oregon ranch at age thirty to see if I could write, and what I found myself writing about was the stark and singular beauty of the high desert that surrounded me—the dusty stones, the oily smell of sagebrush in hot sun, the coyotes and great horned owls and wind from the rimrock whose voices inhabited the night, the sopping snows and muds of February, the dry shell of summer sky and the gray rumbling buildup to a storm, the rimrock flaring red at sundown as the junipers on the hillside stood out in sharp particularity, each with its long slant shadow.

That was the first landscape I ever took the time and spent the energy to begin to know, day to day and month to month, traveling with it through a few turnings of its seasons. It was hard to believe, when I left it, that when I had first arrived in that country it had seemed bleak to me, barren and drab. It takes time, at least a couple of years, to begin to know where you are and to appreciate it for what it is. Transplanted to the hills of the Peninsula, I looked around and many things seemed not quite right—the grass was too brilliantly green in winter, the curving, gray-limbed oaks too sensuously formed for eyes accustomed to spartan pines and shaggy junipers, the honeyed air too sweet with flower scents in spring. But again, I stayed long enough to let the landscape work on me. As some animals in evolutionary time take on the colors of their surroundings, my consciousness has taken on the sights and smells and sounds of its new environment and has begun to make them native to itself. It doesn't require eons, but it does take a couple of years—and a curiosity, a willingness to stand still sometimes, to listen and observe.

Walking the trail through the oaks our first spring here, mid-April, I was baffled night and day by a fine ticking sound in the undergrowth, the sound of very light rain falling from a cloudless sky. I felt nothing on my hands or face, but the sound, though faint, was clear and steady. It took many moments of standing and listening, and kneeling on the trail with my ear next to the poison oak, and staring up at the trees, before I connected what I heard with the sheen of tiny black specks that covered our cars and the gossamer threads that dangled and billowed from the oaks. An insect guide confirmed that I was hearing the industry of oak moth caterpillars, spawned in their millions and chewing their way to maturity up in the trees, raining down their dry excrement in a shower lasting weeks.

Next spring my wife and I listened for the caterpillar rain, and heard it. That and other things we began to notice, some obvious, some as subtle as the invisible rain, became signs for us of the turning year: the poison oak tinging red in mid-August; the golden-crowned sparrows, with their melancholy three-note song, arriving in late September just before the rains; robins and waxwings gorging

on fermented toyon berries in November; the white moths
of January, mustard blooming in late February, woodpeckers drumming incessantly through March; and then the
caterpillar rain, the hills starting to go bleached gold, and
the long blue stillness of summer settling in.

My wife and I don't own this land and didn't build
our cottage. Like great horned owls—very lucky owls—we
found a nest made by others, added a stick or two, and
called it home. But it wasn't home yet. It was only a shelter
on a lovely hillside where we enjoyed ourselves. We began
to realize our home around us, we are realizing it now, by
what we learn to be aware of, what we learn to see and listen
for and come to know as part of our lives.

When we first moved in, we didn't like to walk the
trail at night without a flashlight. From the opening in the
oaks where we park our cars, it rises and falls along a steep
slope for a hundred yards to the cottage door, a tangle of
toyon and poison oak above and below, big live oaks shad-
ing out the stars. On nights of little moon the trail is only
a trace, faintly lighter than the rest of the night, emerging
as the eyes cool down from houselights or headlights. And
some nights—new-moon nights, rainy nights of that thick,
closed-in dark—there is no trail or trace of trail. Caught
then without a light we had a problem, a humbling problem. We would proceed in a slow-motion shuffle, cautiously
sliding one foot forward and then the other, hands held out
against solid dark.

But advancing in that way, gradually, through a year or so of occasional lightless nights, we found our problem becoming an unexpected joy. We found that our feet remember the trail, even if we don't—they know by heart where it narrows, where dirt is loose on the left, that certain stretch where an embedded rock can trip you. They feel their way, judging each placement and correcting, guiding us back to the trail's heart. Something rustles. We wait, listening. The tree crickets, in late summer, surround us in their shimmering gauze of sound. We might catch the flutter of a screech owl up in the limbs. On wet nights we smell the bay laurel as we ease past it, its fragrance bright on the blended background of earth and plant smells. In our blindness, in our slowing down, the trail becomes something more than a passageway. It becomes a place, and we are part of that place, deeply alive and fully present where we cannot stay for long.

In the Navajo language there is no word for changing homes: to relocate is to wither and blow away. For my wife and me, uprooting and replanting ourselves without their five-hundred-year marriage to a region, changing homes must have a meaning if we are to live and not wither. Home for us is not the place we were born, or that perfect somewhere else we used to dream of, but the place where we are —the place we stay long enough to begin to see. It is not a matter of owning the land, or of working the land, but of learning to hold the land in mind, to begin gropingly—

blind on a dark hillside—to imagine ourselves as part of it. We know it imperfectly, not mindfully enough. But here we begin, and when we start over in another place we'll take what we know of this place with us, we'll begin this much closer to home.

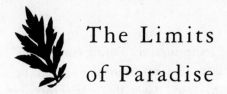

The Limits
of Paradise

ON A PLANET of water the land has to end, and here in the West of North America it ends in prodigal beauty. It ends in mountains plunging to sounds and fjords, in the thunder of calving glaciers, in still forests of the tallest trees on Earth. It ends in rocky stacks haunted by sea lions and gulls, in great waves of sand flowing slowly inland, in heights and dark headlands looming in mist. It ends in coves and strands and bare desert hills, in warm lagoons where gray whales sport and birth their young. And always the land ends in ceaseless barter with wind and waves, in the surge and boom of one of the first musics the planet learned how to make. "Older than man and ages to outlast him," wrote Robinson Jeffers, "the Pacific surf/Still cheerfully pounds the worn granite drum."

Life is richest in the margins, the boundary zones, and nowhere is it richer than along the line where land meets sea. Humans have been drawn to the biotic largess of the Pacific coast for longer than anyone knows, from a time when most of the northern continent was sunk under thousands of feet of ice. They may have arrived by seacraft, following the shoreline south from the Bering land bridge, settling where the ice allowed them, moving on. And, or, they may have come overland, down the ice-free passage known to have existed through what is now British Columbia. One way or another they came and they flourished, sustained by the life of the sea, by the plants and game of forest and meadow, by the rivers thronged with fish.

A second settlement of the coast began not long ago at all—when sails appeared in what Northwest Indians called "the river with one bank," when Junipero Serra and his cohorts trooped up from New Spain to build missions, when trappers opened the country for pelts, and farmers followed for good land and miners for gold. It began and it never stopped. The plenty of the land begot a human plenty, and even as the natural riches declined, the human tide kept pouring in. Those who had used up their chances came seeking the new chance that always lay west, tracking it clear to the last verge of land, where the sun goes down over nothing but sea.

That was the first limit we came to, and the easiest to accept. You don't argue with an ocean. But now we face limits we don't see as well—limits on how we use the land, on what we take from it and ask it to take from us. Here on the sundown shore of North America there are no more territories to light out for, no virgin ground where we might flee our mistakes and start over. Where we are is where we will be—a land as variously beautiful as any on Earth, a land very close to paradise, a land where our chances are slipping away.

The coastal region is not big but long, and last summer I took a long drive to see how it's faring. I started in the temperate rainforest of Vancouver Island, as far north on the coast as it's easy to get by road, and I finished fifteen hundred miles south, among the palms and freeways of Los Angeles. I traveled from one of the world's most elaborate developments of wild nature to one of its most elaborate developments of human beings and their enterprises. Two definite poles, but I found no neat gradient from north to south between them. Up and down the coast, it's clear which kind of development is prevailing.

The western coast of Vancouver Island grows a forest more exuberantly productive than any in the tropics—a dense, moist, silent exclamation of red cedar and hemlock and Sitka spruce. It's a culmination of at least ten thousand years of rain and sun and mild winters, ten thousand years of deepening soils that began with Pleistocene gravels. People have lived in the forest for millennia, yet outside their present villages the signs of their ancestral habitation are few. The only one I could find last summer was a big red cedar with a scar in its side where a ten-foot plank had been split out hundreds of years ago. The tree has continued to grow unharmed, the scar now deep enough that I could stand inside it. In days of driving the Northwest coast, that cedar was the only evidence I saw of sustainable forestry.

There was ample evidence of a different kind of forestry, if that's what it is, a forestry not merely unsustainable but also voracious. The northern and southern thirds of Vancouver Island have been reduced to more stripped earth than woods, laid bare in enormous clearcuts. In the Mackenzie Range, along Highway 4 in the south-center of the island, a government ministry has placed admonishing placards: "Our Forests Are Vital. Please Protect Them." Behind those signs, mile after mile, the view is of mountainsides sheared in long, continuous tracts, burned over and scarred with landslides. A different commentary, less abstract and more attentive to facts, glares in red spray-paint on a bridge rail: "World War III—The War Against The Earth."

The best of what remains of the island's rainforest lies in the Clayoquot Sound region, a domain of mostly undisturbed watersheds and islands being considered for designation as a U.N. biosphere reserve. In 1993, the provincial government announced a management plan that if implemented will leave three-quarters of the Clayoquot rainforest logged or scheduled to be logged. In the spirit of compromise, the government declared that forest fringes will be left intact along the shorelines—only the mountainsides, the scenic backdrops to one of the most dramatic coastlines anywhere, will be stripped of trees. Questions of habitat and biodiversity aside, the government apparently believes that tourists will continue to throng to a coast whose mountains have been tonsured like medieval monks.

The assault on British Columbia's forests is mostly quite legal. Multinational corporations enjoy what amount to perpetual timber leases on public lands, and conservationists have no basis for the kind of litigation their U.S. allies have used so effectively in the Pacific Northwest. They have shown in the past, however, that there are other ways to keep trees from turning into stumps. In 1984, loggers preparing to begin work on Meares Island, just north of road's end in Clayoquot Sound, were met on the water by a flotilla of nonviolent resisters and on the island by an equally nonviolent delegation of Tlaoquiaht Indians who told the loggers they were welcome if their chainsaws stayed in the boat. The Meares Island forest still stands. There and throughout Clayoquot Sound, a committed resistance is fighting for the rainforest, against long odds, as the timber corporations move in.

Meanwhile, across Juan de Fuca and down the Northwest coast, no major watershed has escaped the bite of the saws. South of Olympic National Park, which preserves remnants of a spectacular rainforest, vast stretches of western Washington have been logged at least once. The Oregon Coast Range has been riddled with roads and clearcuts, on public and private lands alike. And the redwood forest of California, home of the tallest living things, has been slashed from two million acres in the eighteenth century to fewer than a hundred thousand scattered acres today. The coastal Northwest wants to be trees, and forest does grow on much of the cut-over ground—a thick woods of alders, mostly, understoried with ferns. Alders are pretty enough, something like aspens, but the forest is dense, dark, and haunted. You can see the big stumps in there. You can feel the ghosts of the old-growth trees.

Our clearcuts are smaller than the Canadian brand, which means they ruin a forest as much by fragmentation as by the mowing itself. Most of the damage doesn't show from the highways, so you have to do one of two things to appreciate it. Fly over, not too high, in a small plane. Or, as I did on my way south, traverse a forest on the logging roads. (I recommend a rental car.) All across the Olympic National Forest, south of the park, I saw little but strips and patches of the original growth, as if a psychopathic barber with an erratic geometrical imagination had gotten to it. The upper slopes, some of them steep as cliffs almost, are banded with multiple road cuts. Soil and stones have spewed downslope in landslides known as puke-outs—an ugly term for an uglier thing. It goes on for forty miles. And every acre, I kept thinking, is public land, owned by us all, part of a system of forest reserves we once set aside —or thought we did—for protection against the timber barons.

Many of the butchered slopes up and down the coast

have been replanted. On steeper ground, the plantations frequently fail. Elsewhere the young Douglas firs have taken hold, and eventually they'll grow into some poor version of a forest—genetically homogeneous, biologically sparse, dull to the eye, and limited in use, the wood suited mainly for pulp. Weyerhaeuser Corporation, which owns a great deal of southwestern Washington, trumpets its replanting achievements in flashy signs—third-growth under way on some tracts, mixed-species stands on others. The "tree-growing people" don't tell you, of course, that they sell at least one-fourth of their logs overseas while mills in the Northwest close down. Or that their profits for 1992, a recession year, were a record $372 million.

Weyerhaeuser and the other industry giants are the only winners in the Northwest timber wars. Having taken almost all of the old growth, many are shifting their attention to the Southeast, where it's quicker and cheaper to grow trees as crops. The land itself has lost immensely, and so have timber workers in the rural Northwest. Pushed out of their jobs by automation, by log exports, by rampant, illegal overcutting in the eighties and the resultant shutdown by lawsuit of the federal forests, they feel angry and betrayed as the region gropes its way to a new economy. On the byways, the back roads where pavement barely holds its own against brambles and alders, I saw the same hand-stenciled sign in front of home after home—"THIS FAMILY SUPPORTED BY TIMBER DOLLARS"—against a backdrop, usually, of hills scalped red-brown or healing with thickets of brush. In Forks, timber capital of the Olympic Peninsula, a storefront poster shows three generations of loggers, including a child, above the caption "Endangered Species."

Those families and businesses blame their troubles on the federal government and on conservation groups. They are mostly right about the former and not entirely wrong about the latter. The Reagan-Bush Forest Service and Bureau of Land Management allowed far more cutting on the public lands than they should have, and Congress repeatedly funded harvests even higher than the agencies requested, thus breeding scores of small mills and logging outfits dependent on an unsustainable cut. We conservationists brought the bad news, in the form of litigation, but we are despised for deeper reasons. We are seen as city dwellers, recreationists who use for pleasure the lands where timber workers live and try to support themselves. To suggest facilely, as some of us have, that they must retrain and relocate, or stay and adapt to a tourist economy, is to tell them that their communities and work skills are irrelevant. In fact, both are essential to the future of the forests. To restore the coastal watersheds will require major work— regrading and restructuring streams, reseeding slopes, reforestation. Not many conservationists know how to run a bulldozer or thin a young forest, but there are timber workers who do, and those workers need jobs.

Like loggers and millhands, commercial fishermen too are out of work these days. In 1993 the coho salmon season was canceled on most of the Oregon coast, and conservationists petitioned the government to list the coho as an endangered species. Salmon trolling was shut down completely between Florence, Oregon, and San Francisco. Salmon runs of all species have plummeted in coastal streams from Puget Sound to Southern California, largely for the same reasons that the spotted owl and marbled murrelet are in trouble. Salmon require watersheds where trees are undisturbed—where they shade the streams and eventually fall, forming pools and trapping gravel the fish need for spawning. Such pristine environments are exceedingly rare on the coast. A century of roading, clearcutting, and urbanization has raised water temperatures, silted the spawning gravels, and triggered violent washouts that have scoured some stream channels down to bedrock. Dams, mines, pollution, diversions for agriculture, and misguided hatchery programs have added further insults to the salmon runs.

As ghosts of big trees haunt the second-growth forests, ghosts of hundred-pound chinook haunt Washington's Elwha River, walled off by two impassable dams early in the century. (Those dams are scheduled for removal—a momentous act of healing, if Congress will appropriate the money.) A ghost run of some four hundred thousand coho throngs the lower Columbia River. Ghost chum salmon run the Klamath and the Sacramento, ghost steelhead in numbers up to twenty thousand a year run the San Diego, the Los Angeles, and stream after other stream in Southern California. Remarkably, a remnant run of steelhead-in-the-flesh still returns to Malibu Creek in Los Angeles County—a testament to the fortitude of their kind and a sign of hope for us all.

Driving south past Tillamook on Oregon's north coast, I remembered watching fall chinook the year before in the headwaters of the Trask River, their great shadowy forms darting and hovering in the rain-dimpled stream as they neared the end of their journey. I felt privileged to watch, and twice privileged later that fall when I hooked my first steelhead. An indomitable power surged against my rod, stripping off line at its pleasure, showing only a deep coppery flash of itself before it threw the hook and left me stunned and shaking in the boat. And grateful. What we've done to the salmonid species is our usual ecological stupidity but more—we've treated these wild lords of the coastal waters with unforgivable disrespect. Their ancestors have been running the rivers of North America for as many as five million years—five million years of pioneering the watersheds, adjusting to volcanic explosions and glacial advances, fertilizing barren gravels and basalts with the rich captured life of the sea. Salmon know their home on this coast with a strength and faithfulness we have scarcely begun to imagine for ourselves.

To protect and restore coastal salmon runs requires one thing above all: to protect and restore their habitat. Endangered species listings, which will multiply in the nineties, are aimed at forcing just that, but they are triggered too late in the process of habitat degradation, when species are already under the shadow of extinction. And, worse, they perpetuate a chronic illusion—that one plant, one animal, one species can be singled out, attended to, and "saved." It's impossible. Depleted salmon runs, like depleted populations of owls and murrelets, are symptoms of a major injury to the ecosystem, the watersheds, the air-water-soil-plant-animal complex that we call the land. If we can heal the land, by leaving it alone where it isn't hurt badly and restoring it where it is, fish and birds and trees will have a reasonable chance of prospering. And so will fishermen and loggers, so will consumers, *if* we accept tighter limits on our extraction and consumption, *if* we accept that the human economy must subject itself to the natural economy that makes it possible.

The Clinton forest plan is a good-faith step in that direction, a step away from the unconscionable policies of the Reagan-Bush years, but it hedges the limits. It does not permanently protect what's left of the old-growth forests, it opens to logging some of the few remaining roadless areas in the Northwestern national forests, and it places insufficient protections around streams and rivers. Similarly, in Southern California, state and federal measures to preserve coastal sage scrub—another old-growth system, one that provides essential habitat for at least fifty species—may be insufficient as well. Much of the scrub has already been lost to malls and subdivisions, and "ecosystem management"— a phrase suddenly on the lips of as many developers and business executives as conservationists—may come to mean nothing more than compromising away what's left, protecting just enough scrub to support a minimal museum-population of the threatened California gnatcatcher. We'll have achieved real ecosystem management when we understand that the essence of management is to preserve ample wild habitat and leave it alone, and to develop the rest with restraint and humility. Humility is a way of acknowledging limits. Jack Ward Thomas, newly appointed chief of the Forest Service, put it this way to President Clinton at last year's Forest Conference: "Ecosystems are more complex than we think. Mr. President, they're more complex than we *can* think."

If the migrations of salmon thread the Pacific coastal region to the open sea, migratory birds weave it into air and join it to their nesting grounds far to the north and their winter ranges in warmer latitudes. The coast itself, from the Skagit River plain on Puget Sound down through San Francisco Bay and the remnant marshes south of Point Conception, guides one current of the seasonal river of birds we call the Pacific Flyway. Another current, a bigger one, follows the

Great Central Valley of California, where settlers in the nineteenth century witnessed flights of ducks and geese that darkened the sky. The valley then was millions of acres of marsh, lakes, vernal pools, and profuse grassland. John Muir, on his way to Yosemite in 1868, waded knee-deep in a wildflower savannah veined with riparian forests, watered by the Sacramento River from the north and the San Joaquin from the south.

Sheep and cattle already were scouring the valley when Muir first saw it, and our century has seen its conversion, by means of the biggest irrigation projects ever engineered, into the richest agricultural region in the history of the world. Where Muir walked in flowers, I drove among endless dead-flat fields of sugar beets, corn, alfalfa, tomatoes, and grain, the water that once raised wild blossoms and lured geese from the sky now captured and systematically conveyed in pumps, pipes, ditches, and bright concrete aqueducts. More than one-fourth of the table food grown in America is grown in these fields. According to Gerald Haslam in *The Great Central Valley: California's Heartland,* the valley's agricultural production in a single year outvalues all the gold mined in California since 1848.

But that stupendous output has exacted stupendous costs. Waterfowl no longer darken the sky or lift from the earth in a storm of wings. "The Pacific Flyway is but a corridor connecting the wetlands of the West," writes Peter Steinhart in *Tracks in the Sky*—and 95 percent of the Central

Valley's wetlands have been drained or otherwise obliterated. Tulare Lake, at flood level once the largest body of fresh water west of the Mississippi, doesn't appear even as a dry lakebed on many road maps. The San Joaquin River, which used to conduct chinook salmon runs into all its tributaries, now disappears along part of its length most years, diverted and sucked dry for the thirsty fields. Water from the Sacramento River, whose valley has half the San Joaquin's arable land and twice its water, is stored, sent south in canals, and pumped uphill for hundreds of miles so that the drier valley can burgeon with grapes, cotton, and rubber tomatoes.

Eighty percent of California's developed water supply is soaked up by agriculture. Federal legislation passed in 1992 designates wildlife, for the first time, as a primary user of Central Valley water. Salmon runs in the Sacramento will benefit, but the law only begins to address the overall pattern of water rapaciousness in the valley. San Joaquin farmers have been pumping groundwater for decades, much faster—half a trillion gallons a year faster—than the aquifers can recharge. Emptied sediment chambers have collapsed, destroying some of the aquifers, and surface land has dropped as much as fifty feet in some places. The farmers drill deeper, at greater expense. In the Salinas Valley, salad bowl to the nation, produce growers and a skyrocketing population are pumping subsurface water so fast that a rapidly advancing saltwater intrusion is less than two miles away from mixing with drinking water sources for the city of Salinas. "We screwed around here for fifty years talking about it," says a member of the Monterey County Water Resources Board. "It's a very distinct possibility that the agriculture industry, which dominates our economy, will go down. Nobody knows how far down."

Salt threatens the valley in another way as well. Through decades of irrigation, natural salts and fertilizer residues have built up in the soil, reaching levels in some areas that have killed the land. Salinization is an inevitable consequence of irrigated agriculture. Ten years ago, Gerald Haslam reports, it had ruined 650,000 acres in the valley. Another million acres could be lost by the end of the century. Like farmers as far back as ancient Mesopotamia, valley growers have tried to solve the problem by installing subsurface tile systems to drain off saline wastewater, but such contrivances work imperfectly, and they only extend the compass of death. In the early 1980s, nests of dead embryos and birds with no eyes and other deformities began to appear at wastewater evaporation ponds in Kesterson National Wildlife Refuge, south of Turlock. Selenium, leached from the bountiful fields, was found to be poisoning the waterfowl. Wastewater throughout the valley—in natural pools, in the San Joaquin River, in the seasonally flooded fields of duck-hunting clubs—bears high levels of selenium and other toxic substances.

At Kesterson, as heads are scratched for a way to clean

the place up, sirens shriek to scare off birds. If they don't scare us, too, we're not as smart as the ducks and geese. The Great Central Valley, like the stripped coastal ranges to the north, has evolved into one colossal exercise in the breaching of limits. Birds and fish suffer first, but as our technological fixes fail to keep up with our hubris, human beings will suffer. Some are suffering already. Because mechanization and large-scale irrigation favor big corporate growers, small farmers are being forced off the land. Their numbers fell by half between 1950 and 1970, and are falling still, documenting once again Wendell Berry's axiom that unsustainable farming depletes people as well as soils.

Cancer and birth defects run high in the valley among farm workers and small-town dwellers alike. One-third of all pesticides manufactured in America are used in the Central Valley—and, like salt in the fields, they don't go away. They're in crops, in water, and in the tule fog that hangs near the ground for weeks at a time in winter. Many growers would rather not use so many chemicals, but they're involved in an agriculture that relies on them and a market that tolerates invisible poisons better than it tolerates high prices or blemished produce. A rice farmer I spoke with in the Sacramento Valley grows a small portion of his crop organically and would like to grow more, but the market isn't there. "When city environmentalists get on me about using chemicals," says Allen Garcia, "I ask them to think about what they buy and what they eat. They've got to help."

Rice farming, long a target of conservationist criticism because it requires much water, is actually one of the brighter spots in Central Valley agriculture. It uses water where the water is—the relatively lush Sacramento Valley —and returns it to the rivers when its work is done. And rice growers like Garcia, in partnership with Ducks Unlimited and other conservation groups, are flooding their fields from fall to spring to re-create some of the wetland habitat the Central Valley has so thoroughly lost. Waterfowl feast on leftover rice and plentiful invertebrates, all the while breaking down rice straw with the action of their feet and depositing their own brand of fertilizer. "Those ducks are paying me dividends," says Garcia with a chuckle. "We're showing we can produce a crop *and* enhance the environment." In a generally discouraging tour of the Central Valley, it gave me a singular lift to encounter a Gary Snyder– quoting rice grower with an Hispanic surname who cites Chinese farming lore three thousand years old while leveling his fields—so they'll require less water—with laser technology.

But if waterfowl habitat is expanding in the valley these days, it depresses farmers and bird-lovers alike that pavement is expanding much faster. The human population here is increasing at two and a half times the rate of the rest of California. Stockton, Modesto, Turlock, and other valley towns are becoming bedrooms of the San Francisco Bay area, sprouting malls, parking lots, and tract home developments in fields where crops once grew. Fresno, according to the

1990 census, is the fastest-growing city in America. The valley as a whole is doing a good job of imitating Los Angeles, and now it has Los Angeles air—a pale brown pall of auto emissions and smoke from agricultural burning, efficiently trapped and held by the Coast Ranges and the Sierra Nevada. Smog is known to be damaging trees in the mountains and crops in the fields. Thousands more acres of productive farmland are turned into asphalt each year. In the words of an old vaquero, quoted in *The Great Central Valley,* "Someday we'll have to plow up the malls to plant something we can eat."

And that brings us, inevitably, to the Los Angeles Basin itself—95 percent of which, I'm told, has been paved, poured with concrete, or otherwise sealed by humanity. I should stipulate that I'm not very fond of Southern California. My life in the West has been lived in the latitudes from San Francisco north. I'm a typically smug resident of Ecotopia, and something happens to me when I cross Tejon Pass and start down in the gravitational pull of the freeways into the appalling dirty-soup air that Edward Abbey likened to mustard gas. It so astounds me that fifteen million people live here and continue to live here, many of them seemingly quite content, that the place seems unreal. I visit in a kind of daze, blinking my watery eyes, and quickly leave.

This time I enter slowly, acclimating myself, making an effort to observe carefully. I poke around the San Gabriel Mountains, where ponderosa pines are visibly sick from ozone in the air, then drive west and south, trying to follow the irregular front lines of suburban sprawl. Tracts of fresh pink stucco houses, newly opened for inspection and purchase, patch the scrubby hills. The slopes are furrowed with erosion gullies. An occasional small oil rig bows and rises, genuflecting to the prevailing god. Around Calabasas, where I spend the night, rows of outsized homes strut their splendor. I stay in a motel called the Country Inn, which stands amid housing developments and commercial strips that only a few years ago *were* country—beautiful country, golden hills studded with oaks. The country survives in a word on a sign, just as the great orchards of the Santa Clara Valley, south of San Francisco, survive mainly as street names such as Apricot Lane and Plum Blossom Drive.

The directory of services I find in my room contains a history of Calabasas, three sentences of which summarize nicely the history of greater Los Angeles. Note the two-word phrase that recurs like a mantra:

> As with most other communities in California, the water supply has always been a huge concern. In 1958 the Las Virgenes Water District was founded, thus assuring the water supply. Continued growth of the area was an immediate result of the plentiful water supply.

I don't know the exact source of this plentiful supply, but other reading has given me some idea. I'm not in L.A. itself, and so the water in my shower does not originate in the Owens Valley, 250 miles away on the east side of the Sierra, robbed fair and square in 1913 by the Los Angeles Water Department and converted from farmland to wasteland. It might come, in part, from local sources. But more of it probably comes from the Colorado River via Parker Dam—which means it derives from glaciers as far away as Colorado and Wyoming—or from the Feather River drainage in Northern California, sent south in the California Aqueduct and launched nearly 2,000 feet over the Tehachapi Mountains to water the growing megalopolis with a genius for ignoring limits.

Try as I might, though, as I think northward I can't muster any regional pride about water issues. San Francisco and the East Bay cities are guilty themselves of plundering far places to assure their own plentiful supplies, and cities in the Northwest, with abundant water close by, take it too much for granted. We in the Portland area began to learn about conservation in the summer of 1992, when a six-year drought brought us to the verge of mandatory controls, but our old habits returned with the rains. The quality of our water is also an issue, because for thirty-five years we have tolerated extensive logging in the watershed near Mount Hood—publicly owned—that supplies the metropolitan area. An old-growth watershed is a natural water storage and filtration system. To clearcut in such a forest is insane in both senses—unclean and crazy—and may result in the need for a two-hundred-million-dollar filtration plant to replace the system we had for free.

Equally insane is our coastal habit, north and south, of using whatever fresh or salt water is handy for a cesspool. The city of Victoria on Vancouver Island flushes twenty million gallons of raw sewage a day into the Strait of Juan de Fuca. Vancouver discharges a much greater volume, treated only at the primary level, into the Strait of Georgia. The rapidly growing Puget Sound communities of western Washington make their own contributions, through overloaded septic systems and sewers that serve both sanitary and storm-water functions, with the result that 40 percent of the sound's commercial shellfish beds are closed because of contamination. Oregon's Willamette River, loading up with sewage, agricultural runoff, and other pollutants, is producing deformed fish again after two decades of relative health. And down here on the south coast, beach closures are occurring in the San Diego area because of raw sewage dumped in the Tijuana River by the city of Tijuana, which has a population of two million and is growing fast.

Toxic industrial discharges are a further insanity. The New River, shared by Mexico and San Diego County, carries enough solvents and heavy metals from Mexican *maquiladoras* (foreign-owned assembly plants in the border region) to qualify as the most polluted river on the North American continent. San Francisco Bay is subjected continually to chemical wastes from refineries, solvents from the so-called clean industries of Silicon Valley, and hydrocarbons washed off the streets and out of the air by rainfall. With more than 75 percent of its wetlands lost to fill and development, and with most of the river flow that once fed and flushed it now diverted for Central Valley agriculture, the bay is becoming a sluggish sink of poisons. Puget Sound is somewhat healthier but suffering the same insults, plus dioxin-forming dyes and bleaches released by paper mills. High rates of liver cancer and reproductive failure occur among bottom fish in several parts of the sound, and recent studies indicate that young salmon merely *passing through* the sound are experiencing growth suppression and impaired immune system function.

But thoughts of pollution are far from my mind the next morning as I hike with a friend in the hills near Topanga Canyon. It's a bright, sun-soft day, the kind of day when it's easy to see why Southern California became the chief attraction of paradise. The chaparral is giving off a sweet fragrance, the fleshy white blooms of the yuccas just popping open. Between us and L.A., the Santa Monica Mountains stand tawny in their heights and green in their clefts, agreeably rugged and wild—wild enough, my friend tells me, to support a population of cougars. (One was seen, not too long ago, beneath a freeway overpass.) Even the infamous L.A. smog seems mild today. It's plainly there— a luminous opalescence in the sky, a smarting in the eyes— but to dwell on it seems a meanspirited quibble on a day so benign and blessed.

In fact, I learn that afternoon in the Sierra Club's West L.A. office that air quality in the basin has improved over the past decade, thanks to better emissions controls on cars, cleaner-burning gasoline, and—very likely—the recession's effect on industrial sources. No one I spoke to was exactly elated, though, since even in its cleaner condition L.A. air was bad enough in 1992 to exceed federal standards for one pollutant or another 180 days of the year. The impact on human health is immeasurable, but it's been estimated that merely meeting federal standards would save nine billion dollars a year in health-related expenses in the greater Los Angeles area. No one has a choice about breathing, and those most susceptible to the ill effects of smog are those with the fewest choices of all—the elderly, the infirm, and young children.

Air quality has been improving in other West Coast cities, too, but as in Los Angeles, there's little cause for celebration. The population of greater Seattle, expanding frenetically the past half decade, may increase another 40 percent by the year 2010, and automobile use—measured in number of trips and vehicle miles traveled—is increasing several times faster. Those numbers mean nothing good for the quality of the Queen City's air, and little is happening there or anywhere on the coast to curb our growing dependence on the automobile. The northern cities that scorn Los Angeles are coming more and more to resemble it, sprawling into far-flung suburbs designed around private auto use, while roads are built and repaired at public expense and public transit languishes. My own little Portland is doing the best of the lot, but even there the freeways are crammed at rush hour, the light rail system is insufficient, and half a million more residents are coming, it's said, in the next twenty years.

All of which is miserably depressing as I begin the long drive home, my time and expense account shot, my head aching with facts and numbers. In the face of the evidence, it's hard to be cheerful about the progress of the human experiment, on this coast or anywhere. Jeffers called humankind a sick microbe, a self-doomed aberration, and in my present mood I can't argue with him—or with the brain scientists who say we're well wired for immediate threats, for fight or flight, but practically incapable of responding to continuous, long-term hazards. And as if to confirm what I'm thinking, brake lights flash and traffic on the Hollywood Freeway congeals to an erratic creep. An accident, the radio reports. And of course this entire sprawling rambleshack village is an accident—a planless accretion of streets and freeways, of suburb after splayed-out suburb, an accidental splurge of millions of souls mostly innocent, wedded to their cars, as I am, trying to make a living, as I am, trying to make it home in the murky light of evening so they can pack the freeways in the morning again for a new day of work.

I've been stuck in this same clog of freeway traffic in every city on the coast, and I always react the same—like an angry child suddenly deprived of his freedom, a freedom whose costs and consequences I don't want to think about but can't help but think about, stewing in fumes on a gridlocked freeway. Somehow, especially in the cities but everywhere, we'll all have to settle for less freedom, or at least a different kind of freedom. However the human brain is wired, we'd better put it to use finding ways to live that don't poison ourselves and everything around us. And while we're at it, we'd better think about how to control our numbers. The fix we're in is twofold, and the Hollywood Freeway this hot summer evening clearly displays it—too many of us fouling our nest, and too many of us period. Growth without limits is disease. Fertility and immigration both contribute to the problem, and it's time to talk about both.

Out of town at last on 101, I think of the reintroduced condors in the Sespe Sanctuary to the north, and I hope they're alive and well tonight. I hope they can thrive in what wild territory we've left them. Around midnight, soothed by hours of country music from Bakersfield, I'm winding up Highway 1 into the Santa Lucias, the Big Sur country, a landscape that never fails to lift me with joy. I park the car and half climb, half slide down a thicketed slope to a broad and grassy moonlit terrace, which I share with a few frightened cows. The steep mountainside plunges below me to the ghostly Pacific surging around rocks, sounding its ancient anthem. This is the last of North America, the very limit of paradise, but it is also a beginning, always a beginning. Here, out of the windy chaos of possibility, a continent rises into being—mute, noble, unspeakably beautiful, and we unspeakably privileged to share it. *The world's well made,* wrote the hawk-faced poet, and despite the prophecies of his darker hours, we are well made, too. We are arrogant, shortsighted, not nearly as intelligent as we think we are, but we are capable of nobility and generosity ourselves, and surely we are competent to live here if we will try. Below me the Pacific foams and surges, bearing its power from chartless reaches, as wild and perennial as hope itself.

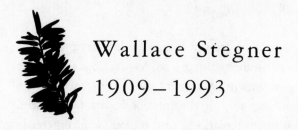

Wallace Stegner
1909–1993

"SOMETHING WILL HAVE gone out of us as a people if we ever let the remaining wilderness be destroyed; if we permit the last virgin forests to be turned into comic books and plastic cigarette cases; if we drive the few remaining members of the wild species into zoos or to extinction; if we pollute the last clear air and dirty the last clean streams and push our paved roads through the last of the silence, so that never again will Americans be free in their own country from the noise, the exhausts, the stinks of human and automotive waste. And so that never again can we have the chance to see ourselves single, separate, vertical and individual in the world, part of the environment of trees and rocks and soil, brother to the other animals, part of the natural world and competent to belong in it . . .

"We simply need that wild country available to us, even if we never do more than drive to its edge and look in. For it can be a means of reassuring ourselves of our sanity as creatures, a part of the geography of hope."

241

Those words are from a letter Wallace Stegner wrote in 1960 to a researcher studying wilderness preservation for the federal government. A copy of the letter came into the hands of then secretary of the interior Stuart Udall, who interrupted his own remarks to read it aloud at a conference on wilderness in San Francisco. The proceedings of the conference were made into a Sierra Club book, and during the late 1960s a copy of the book happened into my life. I was eighteen or nineteen, fresh from the East, trying to be a student at Reed College in Portland. I skimmed among the book's contents, finding much of interest, but it was Wallace Stegner's letter-essay, then called "The Wilderness Idea," now called "Wilderness Letter," that took me by force. I had always been drawn to the outdoors, as a hiker and fisherman back East, and more recently as a climber. And I had always been drawn to words and ideas, the sounds of language, the heft and smells of books. I loved both worlds, but they seemed almost entirely separate.

Now here was a man writing what clearly was literature—writing with measured passion, with gravity and spirit, with knowledge of history, geography, American authors—and nature, wild nature, was his very subject. It was big news to me that a writer could do that. I had read parts of *Walden,* like any high schooler, but Thoreau and I hadn't connected—because his language seemed archaic, maybe, or maybe because he was taught in school. "Wilderness Letter" found me on the loose in the West, and it showed me that the landscapes I was getting to know had significance beyond their natural beauty and their service as my recreational playground. Wallace Stegner made me see that wilderness is all interfused with what it means to be an American. Wilderness shaped our history, and though we no longer live in it, it lives in us, as hope and enthusiasm. If we destroy it, we destroy one of the deep springs of our vitality.

"Wilderness Letter" is one of the great written defenses of North America's wild nature. Has it changed minds? Today we have a Wilderness Act and a National Wilderness Preservation System. Wallace Stegner's conservation writing unquestionably aided that birth, not by changing minds from one side of the issue to the other—writing can't do that, not even the best—but by instilling its passionate reason in the minds of those with similar stirrings, but inarticulate. Wallace Stegner did not change my mind on wilderness. He formed it. "Wilderness Letter" and other of his essays gave my thoughts a place to stand, and a light by which to see.

Years later, when I found the will and discipline to become a writer, his phrases mixed with others in the compost of my reading to give me something else—the beginnings of a style. I liked the way he sounded on the page. I liked the dignity, the authority, the sense he gives of having important things to say and the patience and wherewithal to get them said. The style is formal, but lively with

colloquial energy, too. It is personal without being con-
fessional. It points beyond itself to the worthy and en-
during things of this world, those of the human realm and
those of nature, and values those above its own powers and
virtuosity.

The character of the writing, not surprisingly, resem-
bled the character of the man. In 1982 I went to Stanford
University, as a poet, on a fellowship bearing Wallace Stegner's name. When the fellowship led to a lecturer's job and
I needed a place to live, the director of the creative writing
program told me that Wallace and Mary Stegner might
have a small house for rent on their property in Los Altos
Hills. They did—a redwood-sided cottage, just down the
hill from their own house, with a native oak forest on one
side and an open field of wild oats and mustard on the other.
My wife and I lived there five years, as tenants, as paid
helpers around the place, and as friends.

The cottage had once been Wally's writing study. A
floor-to-ceiling living room window looked out on the fo-
liage and smooth gray limbs of live oaks—the same oaks,
it pleased me to think, that the author of "Wilderness
Letter" must have looked upon some two decades before. A
hundred-yard trail led from the cottage to our parking area,
passing just below the Stegners' deck and Wally's new
study. Marilyn and I became accustomed to hearing the
steady tap of his Olympia manual typewriter as we walked
the trail in the morning. That was his call, and it began as

early in the day almost as the birds began theirs. Once in a while a whiff of cigar smoke hung in the air, blending with the scent of bay laurels.

The tall, silver-haired man we began to know was considerate and friendly from the start, but his dignified reticence and my own awed reticence made conversation sparse for a while. I feared that anything of substance I tried to say would betray my considerable dearth of learning, and to make small talk with such a man, unless he began it, seemed disrespectful. Then one morning he put me at ease in a way he couldn't have intended. Walking the trail below his study, I noticed the typewriter was silent. A different noise, a rainlike patter, made me look up, and there was the eminent author, relieving himself over the rail of his deck. It was one of the few times I ever saw him disconcerted, but even then he wasn't much bothered. "Welcome to the country," he said with a grin. "We're not very formal."

I'm told that Wallace Stegner could present a forbidding face in his teaching years, and I believe it, but Marilyn and I saw mostly his smile. It came easily and often to his face, the lines of his age all participating, his eyes lit with equal measures of delight and mischief. I remember him smiling with pleasure at my stepson's talent for soothing a lizard into riding his bare shoulder. I remember him tossing his trowel toward the corner of the yard where he wanted to work next, and grinning to himself when it landed beside

ght shrub. And I remember Marilyn talking with a
end, Tanya Berry, about a certain sly sparkle they saw in
Wally's eyes. They agreed he was extraordinarily attractive.

"Really," I said. "So he stands out among older men?"

"No, my dear," replied my wife. "He stands out
among *men*."

Poised and dignified as Wallace Stegner was, when he
smiled you could always see the sensuous little savage, as
he called the boy he had been, who started out on the
Saskatchewan plains a long time ago. It was in that vast and
windy land, with the nearest neighbor four miles away,
with the great sky curving clear to the ground in every
direction, with mice and coyotes and burrowing owls for
brothers, it was there that he first came to a sense of himself
as a human being, and it was there that his passion for
wilderness first was stirred. Not the idea of wilderness, but
the land itself in its wild immensity. In his essay "The Gift
of Wilderness," he describes a defining moment that occurred in 1915, when he was six, crossing the empty prairie
in a wagon with his father and brother to build a house on
their homestead:

"Then in the night I awoke, not knowing where I was.
Strangeness flowed around me; there was a current of cool
air, a whispering, a loom of darkness overhead. In panic I
reared up on my elbow and found that I was sleeping beside
my brother under the wagon, and that a night wind was
breathing across me through the spokes of the wheel. It

came from unimaginably far places, across a vast emptiness, below millions of polished stars. And yet its touch was soft, intimate, and reassuring, and my panic went away at once. That wind knew me. I knew it. Every once in a while, sixty-six years after that baptism in space and night and silence, wind across grassland can smell like that to me, as secret, perfumed, and soft, and tell me who I am."

Reading the *Collected Stories* a few years ago, I noticed that nearly half of them are told from a boy's or young man's point of view. Wallace Stegner realized that point of view better than any other writer I know of, and he was capable of that because he and the sensuous little savage never parted. Through all his years and all his words, he gave the boy life in his art, and the boy gave life to him. And through the boy those big windy plains, and the Rockies and the Wasatch Front, the slickrock country of the Colorado Plateau, the Great Basin and the snowy Sierra— through the boy it was the wilderness West that gave Wallace Stegner his indomitable spirit, that energized his prodigious writing career that lasted from the 1930s into the 1990s.

He relished his work, and not only the work in his study. Usually his writing for the day was done by late morning, and most afternoons he devoted to the place, the home on a hill where he and Mary lived for nearly half a century. Together they humanized the foothill landscape in ways that left the wildness in it. Native oaks and planted pines grew up around their pale green house; they built their deck around one of the oaks. They kept their beds and hedges in an easeful kind of order—nothing regimented, nothing cropped in hard lines. Deer and the occasional fox or coyote passed among their shrubs and citrus trees. Wally did make war on gophers, whose insults to the grounds he found insufferable. And he claimed to have knocked off loudmouth jays with his pellet gun, but I didn't believe him.

He would move from task to task around the place, weeding here and fertilizing there, pruning the roses, rooting out a shot lemon tree and planting another, spading a new bed in the impossible dobe soil. There was only a week in the spring and a week in the fall when you could work that soil, he grumped—the rest of the year it was sodden clay or baked brick. At age seventy-seven, the year *Crossing to Safety* came out, he built a tool shed almost single-handedly. "Such as she is, such as she may become . . . ," I heard him intoning one day as he banged nails. Outdoor work seemed to bring out the poetry in him. When I'd pass by on my chores, he'd often have a few lines of Frost or Wordsworth for me. Once I found him declaiming a version of Milton about a gopher he'd trapped. "Which way he flies is hell," sang Wally, unimpaling the rodent and tossing him to the field. *"Himself* is hell, foul vermin . . ."

There was a particular kind of work he called "idiot's delight"—clipping the leaves off small prunings from the

248

trees, then clipping those twigs and shoots into thin sticks of kindling. Despite his name for it, he enjoyed that work. With the Giants on the radio if they were playing, he'd stand shirtless in the sun and clip his way through an afternoon, turning debris that I would have dumped in the field into fuel that would dry through the months and warm his study on chill winter mornings. When the woodbox was full, he'd start heaps here and there like pack-rat nests. He was a man who took little for granted, who wasted nothing, but idiot's delight told more of him than frugality. It was one of his ways of recharging, of letting the pool replenish. And, I gradually came to see, all that clipping and storing was a novelist's work, a long-timer's work—the work of a man who knew the labors of countless mornings, cold fingers hitting the typewriter keys, the fireplace returning the small saved warmth of days gone by.

He was working on the back terrace one afternoon, pulling up sagging bricks and resetting them in sand, when I came home from teaching and joined him. For several minutes I did more talking than work. It was a bad day and a bad quarter; I was teaching more than I was used to and feeling kind of frazzled. How, I complained, could I finish my manuscript of poems? How could I write new work? I had no time, no energy left over.

Wallace Stegner answered my complaint with the most profound rebuke I have ever received. He spoke as generously as he could. Kneeling to his work, smoothing the sand and carefully setting each brick, he gave me the lasting benefit of his silence. He allowed me to realize, with no word from him, that no word was needed. His example was answer enough—he who had finished *The Big Rock Candy Mountain* snowbound in an underheated Vermont cabin, on unpaid leave from Harvard, writing reviews and what he called potboilers to support his family as he threw himself at the novel seven days a week. No one made time for Wallace Stegner to write. He made it himself, just as he made time to clip twigs into kindling, just as he made time to tap and settle old bricks into sand as carefully as he crafted a paragraph.

There was a way he had of shuffling along in a deliberate kind of hurry, hose or rake or flowerpot in hand, his torso tilted forward, feet keeping close to the ground. It was eager and careful at the same time. Since he died I've been seeing him walk that way, and I've been thinking of all he got done in an afternoon, shuffling from orchids to carport to pool to pyracantha, slipping into his study maybe once for a quick flurry at the typewriter. And I've been thinking of all he got done in a lifetime, too—how he shuffled around the West as a boy, shuffled on through schools and jobs to the work of writing, from Utah and Iowa to Wisconsin and Cambridge, Vermont to California, California to Vermont, Rockies and Great Basin to Los Altos Hills, from word to word, and sentence to sentence, and page to page. Look at all he made, in his slow hurry, by the time he was done.

250

"You don't go there to find something," he once said about wilderness, "you go there to disappear." Now Wallace Stegner has disappeared into the wildness of the world he loved. Few men and few women will leave more of themselves to the living. Now the writing must stand for the writer—his stone, his witness, his generous bequest. His epitaph might come from any number of his pages. For me it is a passage from the title piece of *The Sound of Mountain Water*. An eleven-year-old from the dryland prairie is standing beside his first mountain river, in the Yellowstone country. A man is looking back to write about the river, and about the boy, and by the time he comes to his final paragraph, he is writing a portrait of his own spirit:

"By such a river it is impossible to believe that one will ever be tired or old. Every sense applauds it. Taste it, feel its chill on the teeth: it is purity absolute. Watch its racing current, its steady renewal of force: it is transient and eternal. And listen again to its sounds: get far enough away so that the noise of falling tons of water does not stun the ears, and hear how much is going on underneath—a whole symphony of smaller sounds, hiss and splash and gurgle, the small talk of side channels, the whisper of blown and scattered spray gathering itself and beginning to flow again, secret and irresistible, among the wet rocks."

Notes

In writing these essays I've drawn on the knowledge and imagination of many people, both through conversation and through reading. All of the sources I mention below were useful, and some were indispensable.

THE GARDEN AND THE FIELD
The Robert Frost poem quoted, indirectly, on page 1 is "Putting in the Seed," and the poem directly quoted on page 6 is Frost's "Mending Wall." On page 5 I refer to Theodore Roethke's "Cuttings (later)." As for Cotton Mather (page 15), see "Place of Wild Beasts" and the notes to that essay.

PACK RAT
The guidebook mentioned on page 26 is *The Audubon Society Field Guide to North American Mammals* by John O. Whitaker, Jr.

THE IMPOVERISHMENT OF SIGHTSEEING

For those who haven't sampled Edward Abbey's views on automobiles and other topics, the place to begin is *Desert Solitaire.* You won't be sorry.

ON THE POWER OF WILD WATER

My epigraph is the last paragraph of "Overture: The Sound of Mountain Water," in *The Sound of Mountain Water* by Wallace Stegner. Thoreau's Harvard commencement address can be found in the "Early Essays and Miscellanies" volume of the Princeton edition of the *Writings of Henry D. Thoreau.* The first Thoreau quotation on page 52 is from *Walden,* chapter 5 ("Solitude"), and the one on page 53 is from *The Maine Woods.* The two sentences on page 54 are from the *Journal,* July 11, 1851. A good way into the *Journal* is Laurence Stapleton's selection, *H. D. Thoreau: A Writer's Journal.*

Thomas Ewbank (page 51) is quoted by Russel B. Nye in chapter 6 of *This Almost Chosen People,* and by Donald Worster in chapter 2 of *Nature's Economy.* Ewbank's magnum opus, published in 1855, is titled *The World A Workshop: or The Physical Relationship of Man to the Earth.*

For information on the nature and history of the Klamath River Canyon, I have relied on the *Final Eligibility and Suitability Report for the Upper Klamath Wild and Scenic*

River Study, published by the Bureau of Land Management (U.S. Department of the Interior) in 1990.

Roger Hamilton, one of the Klamath River's best friends, provided the occasion for writing the speech that became this essay and helped me greatly in getting my facts straight.

PLACE OF WILD BEASTS

I'm indebted to *Wilderness and the American Mind,* by Roderick Nash, for background and several particular facts. Readers wishing a detailed historical treatment of American attitudes toward wild nature will find it in Nash's book.

The words of Cotton Mather are from *The Wonders of the Invisible World* (1693). (All italics are his.) Mather is so busy sniffing out the devil's ploys that he sees *this* world scarcely at all, while Thomas Morton, despite his exploiter's mind, sees nature clearly and writes engagingly about it. His *New English Canaan* (1637), from which I quote on pages 60–61, contains some of the first descriptions of New World flora and fauna.

Thoreau's statement on page 61 is from chapter 17 ("Spring") of *Walden.* The passage it's taken from is one of the great defenses of wilderness. Wallace Stegner's "Wilderness Letter," the central idea of which I characterize on pages 70–71, is another; it's in *The Sound of Mountain Water* and many anthologies. To read the Wilderness Act of 1964, which was written by the conservationist Howard Zahniser and is itself a fine piece of prose, see *The Wilderness Act Handbook,* available from the Wilderness Society.

For information on recreational impacts on wilderness, I thank Steve Sorseth, Margaret Peterson, and Steve Couche of the U.S. Forest Service. Bob Bachman of the Forest Service, Tony Basabe of the Huxley College of Environmental Studies at Western Washington University, and C. L. Rawlins of Boulder, Wyoming, all helped me with information on air quality and wilderness. Much of my paragraph on global warming and the West I owe to Ronald P. Neilson of Oregon State University.

THE LONG DANCE OF THE TREES

My characterization of the old-growth Douglas fir ecosystem (pages 79–83) draws heavily on two publications of the U.S. Forest Service: *Ecological Characteristics of Old-Growth Douglas-Fir Forests,* by Jerry Franklin and others, and *The Seen and Unseen World of the Fallen Tree,* by Chris Maser and James M. Trappe. Conversations with Jerry Franklin and Chris Maser were very helpful. I also found useful information in part one of *Western Forests,* an Audubon field guide by Stephen Whitney, and in *The Fragmented Forest* by Larry D. Harris.

Some of the history on pages 84–85, and the John Smith quotation, are from Russel B. Nye's *This Almost Chosen People.* Rick Brown of the National Wildlife Federation, James Monteith and Wendell Wood of the Oregon Natural Resources Council, and Jean Durning, Bob Freimark, Jeff Olson, Larry Tuttle, and Jay Watson, all of the Wilderness Society, were friendly and knowledgeable informants. Chuck Sisco of the Audubon Society proved an excellent guide to both old-growth forest and good huckleberries.

The Reagan administration official (page 78) is quoted by Bill Devall and George Sessions in *Deep Ecology*. The John Muir passage on pages 83–84 is from *John of the Mountains,* the one on page 90 from "A Wind-Storm in the Forests," in *The Mountains of California*. Aldo Leopold's words on page 91 I take from "Pines Above the Snow," in *A Sand County Almanac*. In the last paragraph of the essay I allude to the first chapter of Ralph Waldo Emerson's *Nature*.

THE MACHINE AND THE GROVE

For biocentrism and the ideas of deep ecology, begin with *Deep Ecology* by Devall and Sessions. For more on Earth First! see *Ecodefense: A Field Guide to Monkeywrenching,* published by Ned Ludd Books of Tucson, and Dave Foreman's *Confessions of an Eco-Warrior*. The writings of Dr. Martin Luther King, Jr., have been collected in several books. "Letter from Birmingham Jail," in *Why We Can't Wait,* is an eloquent defense of nonviolent direct action.

The Gary Snyder stanzas on page 103 are from his

poem "Front Lines," in *Turtle Island*. The Bob Dylan lyric on the same page is from "Absolutely Sweet Marie" *(Blonde on Blonde)*. I thank Andy Kerr of the Oregon Natural Resources Council for information on the history of the Bald Mountain dispute.

AMONG ANIMALS

The Denise Levertov quotation on page 112 is from her poem "Come into Animal Presence," in *The Jacob's Ladder* and *Poems 1960–1967*. Aldo Leopold's statement on page 114 is the first sentence of his foreword to *A Sand County Almanac*. The journals of Lewis and Clark are lively and often moving; a good recent edition is *The Journals of Lewis and Clark*, edited by Frank Bergon. William Bartram's *Travels* contains fine passages amid much florid effusion.

For data on extinct and threatened species, I'm indebted to the Endangered Species Office of the U.S. Fish and Wildlife Service, and to *The Last Extinction*, edited by Les Kaufman and Kenneth Mallory. Donald Griffin's books are clearly written and persuasive; *Animal Thinking* is still in print. Darwin's views on the continuity of mental life between animals and humans can be found in *The Descent of Man* and *The Expression of the Emotions in Man and Animals*. David Snyder of Austin Peay State University read a draft of this essay and helped me on several points of fact and clarity.

The Zuni story, which is titled "The Boy and the Deer," must be read out loud for its full impact to be felt. It's a great work of tragedy, and the other stories in Dennis Tedlock's *Finding the Center* are nearly as good.

DESERT WALKING
The "greatest friend and lover of these canyons," to whom I refer on page 143, was, of course, Edward Abbey.

MARKS ON THE LAND
I learned much about rock art from *Spirit Windows: Native American Rock Art of Southeastern Utah* by Joe Pachak and Winston B. Hurst. For a detailed treatment by an acknowledged expert in the field, see Polly Schaafsma's *Indian Rock Art of the Southwest.* Pat Welch of the Bureau of Land Management was a good guide to the geoglyphs, and helpful too was Boma Johnson's *Earth Figures of the Lower Colorado and Gila River Deserts: A Functional Analysis.* Stephen Hamilton took time from his digs to steer me away from several errors.

REMEMBERING THE SACRED FAMILY
Payatamu's story, titled "The Women and the Man," can be found in Dennis Tedlock's *Finding the Center.* The Wasco story of the boy and the spirit Elk is called "The

Elk, the Hunter, and the Greedy Father." *Coyote Was Going There,* compiled and edited by Jarold Ramsey, contains that and many other fine stories from Native American cultures of the Northwest. *Black Elk Speaks,* though probably flavored considerably by the personal beliefs of its translator, is a book of great beauty and wisdom.

I quote and characterize Aldo Leopold's ideas from "The Land Ethic," in *A Sand County Almanac.* To pursue Wendell Berry's views on Christianity and ecological responsibility, see "The Gift of Good Land," in his book of the same title, and "God and Country," in *What Are People For?* The Gaia hypothesis, developed by James Lovelock, can be explored in his two books, *Gaia: A New Look at Life on Earth* and *The Ages of Gaia.*

THE POEM OF BEING

I've taken information about mass extinctions from articles by William Glen ("What Killed the Dinosaurs?" *American Scientist,* July–August 1990) and Stephen Jay Gould ("An Asteroid to Die For," *Discover,* October 1989). For background and much information on Charles Darwin, the history of the universe, and other subjects, I thank Timothy Ferris for his packed and accessible *Coming of Age in the Milky Way.*

"Poetics," the poem by A. R. Ammons from which I take my epigraph, is in both the original and expanded editions of his *Selected Poems.* Rilke's "wise blindness" is quoted by Norman O. Brown in *Life Against Death.* W. S. Di Piero's words I quote from "Francis Bacon and the Fortunes of Poetry" in his book *Out of Eden: Essays on Modern Art.*

All of Whitman's lines are from "Song of Myself" in the 1892 edition of *Leaves of Grass.* The long Robinson Jeffers excerpt on pages 188–89 is from "Birds and Fishes," one of his last and best poems. The shorter passage that follows is from "The Answer." Both can be found in *Rock and Hawk: A Selection of Shorter Poems by Robinson Jeffers,* compiled and edited by Robert Hass. That book, not the earlier *Selected Poetry* or *Selected Poems,* is the best representation of Jeffers.

THE LIMITS OF PARADISE

Vicki Husband and Sharon Chow, both of the Sierra Club of Western Canada, provided me with information on the temperate rainforest and its plight. I'm also grateful to Lighthawk, the environmental air force, for showing me the destruction from above, and to Adrian Dorst, knowledgeable guide and dedicated protector of the rainforest. A fuller treatment than I had room for in this essay can be found in my article "The Canadian Cut" in the Fall 1988 issue of *Wilderness.*

For their help on forest and salmon issues in the Northwest, I thank Bill Arthur and Julia Reitan of the Sierra Club's Northwest office; Bob Freimark of the Wilderness Society's Portland office; and Tim McKay of the North Coast Environmental Center in Arcata, California. An essential source is "Pacific Salmon at the Crossroads," in *Trout,* Winter 1992. *Wild Fish,* published by the Wilderness Society and edited by Valerie Kitchen, is an invaluable journal of the campaign to save native salmonids. See also my "Dance of Denial" in the March–April 1993 issue of *Sierra.*

Gerald Haslam's comprehensive book, with photographs by Robert Dawson and Stephen Johnson, was my principal source for the section on the Central Valley of California. Peter Steinhart's *Tracks in the Sky,* with photographs by Tupper Ansel Blake, is an informative and beautifully written account of the Pacific Flyway. On water issues I'm indebted to David Fullerton, of the Natural Heritage Institute in San Francisco, and to T. H. Watkins, for his chapter in *The Water Hustlers.* I learned much about wetlands from Jackie McCort, of the Sierra Club's Northern California field office, and from Allen Garcia, rice farmer and spokesperson for the Northern California Water Association. *A Natural History of California,* by Allan A. Schoenherr, was a useful source.

The Clean Air Coalition, the American Lung Association, and the Southern California Air Quality Management District all provided information on air quality in the Los Angeles Basin. Larry Freilich and others in the Sierra Club's Southern California field office were very helpful, as were

Tim Frank of the club's Los Padres chapter and Walt Tunnessen of the San Diego chapter. Two individuals in Seattle were especially enlightening on issues of air quality, water quality, and urban development in the Northwest: Kathy Fletcher, of People for Puget Sound, and Preston Schiller, of the Institute for Transportation and the Environment.

The lines by Robinson Jeffers I quote in the first paragraph are from "Gray Weather," and the partial line I've italicized in the final paragraph is from "Autumn Evening." Both poems can be found in *Rock and Hawk: A Selection of Shorter Poems by Robinson Jeffers,* compiled and edited by Robert Hass. John Muir's accounts of flower-wading in the Central Valley are in *The Yosemite* and *The Mountains of California.*

WALLACE STEGNER

"Wilderness Letter" and "The Sound of Mountain Water" are collected in *The Sound of Mountain Water.* "The Gift of Wilderness" is in *One Way to Spell Man.*

The Sierra Club book I mention in the third paragraph is *Wilderness: America's Living Heritage,* edited by David Brower and published in 1961.

This essay grew out of two speeches: one given at the memorial service for Wallace Stegner at Stanford University, May 3, 1993, and the other as part of A Tribute to Wallace Stegner, University of Portland, October 10, 1993.

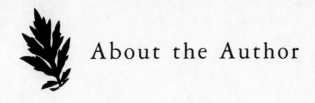

About the Author

BORN IN SOUTH CAROLINA and raised in the suburbs of Washington, D.C., John Daniel came West in 1966 and stayed. He has worked as a college student, logger, railroad inspector, rock climbing instructor, hod carrier, and poet-in-the-schools. In 1982 he received a Wallace Stegner Fellowship in Poetry at Stanford University, where he then taught for five years as a lecturer in creative writing and composition. Daniel is poetry editor of *Wilderness* Magazine and the author of two books of poems, *Common Ground* (Confluence Press, 1988) and *All Things Touched by Wind* (Salmon Run Press, 1994). He and his wife, Marilyn, an environmental engineer, live near Eugene, Oregon. *The Trail Home* won the Oregon Book Award for Creative Nonfiction in 1993.